TYPE 2 DIABETES COOKBOOK

365 Days of Healthy and Tasty Recipes to Take Care of Your Well-Being Without Giving Up the Foods You Love

Allison Lawrence

Table of Contents

Conversion Tables 10

Breakfast 13

   1.   Breakfast Parfait 13

   2.   French Toast Sticks 13

   3.   Omelet with Cheeses and Tomato 13

   4.   Chia Seed With Nuts and Pomegranate 14

   5.   Smoothie With Mango, Apple, Spinach, and Muesli 14

   6.   Porridge With Walnuts 14

   7.   Coconut Pancakes 14

   8.   Banana Barley Porridge 15

   9.   Apple Filled Swedish Pancake 15

   10.   Blueberry Muffin Loaf 15

   11.   Cheese Spinach Waffles 16

   12.   Potatoes, Chicken Sausage, and Egg 16

   13.   Apple & Cinnamon Pancake 16

   14.   Buckwheat Grouts Breakfast Bowl 17

   15.   Cinnamon and Coconut Porridge 17

   16.   Steel-Cut Oatmeal Bowl with Fruit and Nuts 17

   17.   Apple Dumplings 17

   18.   Eggs and Ham 18

   19.   Chocolate Pudding Pies 18

   20.   Walnut and Oat Granola 18

   21.   Coconut and Berry Oatmeal 19

   22.   Cottage Pancakes 19

   23.   Buckwheat Crêpes 19

   24.   Banana Crêpe Cakes 20

Snacks and Appetizers 21

   25.   Ham and Goat Cheese Omelet 21

   26.   Bacon and Mushroom Bite-Size Quiche 22

   27.   Rice Cakes with Fire Jelly 22

   28.   Pesto Cauliflower 22

29. Roasted Italian Green Beans & Tomatoes 22

30. Baked Omelet Mix 23

31. Zucchini Mini Pizzas 23

32. Marinated Mushroom Wraps 23

33. Grilled Peaches 24

34. Dark Chocolate Almond Yogurt Cups 24

35. Lemon Fat Bombs 24

36. Tiramisu Shots 25

37. Choco Peppermint Cake 25

38. Low-Carb Biscuits 25

39. Aromatic Toasted Pumpkin Seeds 25

40. Apple Pita Pockets 26

41. Cinnamon Rolls 26

42. Parsley Chicken Breast 26

43. Almond Coconut Biscotti 27

44. BLT Stuffed Cucumbers 27

45. Cheese Crisp Crackers 27

46. Chili Lime Tortilla Chips 27

Poultry 29

47. Mustard Chicken 29

48. Sticky Chicken 29

49. Stuffed Chicken Breasts 30

50. Oven Parmesan Chicken 30

51. Chicken with Caper Sauce 30

52. Chicken Enchilada Spaghetti Squash 31

53. Creamy and Aromatic Chicken 31

54. Roasted Chicken With Root Vegetables 32

55. Mu Shu Chicken 32

56. Country-Style Wedge Salad With Turkey 33

57. Balsamic Chicken 33

58. Buffalo Chicken and Cheese Meatballs 33

59. Turkey Scaloppini 34

60. Garlic Chicken 34

Red Meat 35

61. Pepper Steak Stew 35

62. Greek Lamb Salad 35

63. Braised Lamb with Carrots 36

64. Beef, Artichoke & Mushroom Stew 36

65. Italian Beef 37

66. Skirt Steak With Peanut Sauce 37

67. Brisket With Cauliflower 37

68. Butter Beef and Spinach 38

69. Low-fat Steak 38

70. Steak Sandwich 38

71. Coffeed and Herbed Steak 39

72. Roasted Beef with Shallot Sauce 39

73. Open-Faced Pub-Style Bison Burgers 39

74. Broccoli Beef Stir-Fry 40

75. Slow-Cooker Roast with Green Beans 40

76. Baked Macaroni with Red Sauce 40

Vegetables and Salads 43

77. Spinach Rolls 43

78. Swiss Chard with Raisins & Pine Nuts 43

79. Diced Vegetable Salad 43

80. Broccoli and Bacon Salad 44

81. Chopped Veggie Salad 44

82. Harvest Salad 44

83. Layered Salad 45

84. Pickled Cucumber and Onion Salad 45

85. Pomegranate and Brussels Sprouts Salad 45

86. Eggplant Surprise 45

87. Pumpkin Custard 46

88. Mushroom and Cauliflower Risotto 46

89. Peppers with Sriracha Mayo 46

90. Spinach Rich Ballet 47

91. Quinoa and Lush Vegetable Bowl 47

92. Avocado White Bean Sandwich 47

Pork Recipes 48

93. Jamaican Pork Tenderloin 48

94. Pork Ribs 48

95. Pork Loin Roulades 49

96. Roasted Pork and Apples 49

97. Irish Pork Roast 49

98. Cranberry Pork Roast 50

99. Crock Pork Tenderloin 50

100. Barbecue Pork Chops 50

101. Lime Pulled Pork 50

102. Mustard Pork Chops 51

103. Citrus Pork Tenderloin 51

104. Pork Loin with Carrots 51

105. Pork and Apple Skillet 52

106. Pineapple Pork Tacos 52

Fish and Seafood **53**

107. Tuna with Olives 53

108. Stuffed Swordfish 54

109. Pesto Fish Fillet 54

110. Shrimp Zoodles 54

111. Mediterranean Fish 55

112. Garlicky Shrimp 55

113. Feta Tomato Sea Bass 55

114. Codfish with Shrimp 56

115. Tartar Tuna Patties 56

116. Fresh Rosemary Trout 56

117. Blackened Shrimp 56

118. Cilantro Lime Grilled Shrimp 57

119. Seared Sesame Tuna Steak 57

120. Alfredo Shrimp 57

121. Tilapia with Coconut Rice 58

122. Grilled Tuna Kebabs 58

123. Chili Lime Cod 58

124. Sesame-Crusted Tuna with Green Beans 59

Soups **60**

125.	Carrot Ginger Soup	60
126.	Mushroom Soup	61
127.	Vegetable Beef Soup	61
128.	7-Minutes Egg Drop Soup	61
129.	Classic Tomato Soup	61
130.	Creamy Tomato Soup	62
131.	Fresh Broccoli Soup	62
132.	Low Carb Cream Bouillon	62
133.	Mashed Peas Goulash	63

Lunch and Dinner 64

134.	Pork Chops with Apples and Red Cabbage	64
135.	Coconut Flour Tortillas	64
136.	Beer Bread	64
137.	Chickpea Soup	65
138.	Butter Sautéed Green Beans	65
139.	Tender Veggie Spring Peas	65
140.	Eggplant and Bulgur Pilaf	65
141.	Filled Chicken Breast	66
142.	Onion and Zucchini Platter	66
143.	Ginger Soup	66
144.	Creamy Chicken	66
145.	Chicken Tortilla Soup	67
146.	Beef Salad	67

Sauces and Dressing 68

147.	Alfredo Sauce	68
148.	Sriracha Peanut Sauce	68
149.	Salsa de Queso	69
150.	Aioli	69
151.	Sriracha Mayonnaise	69
152.	Ketchup	69
153.	Ranch Dressing	70
154.	Italian Vinaigrette	70
155.	Lemony Dill and Yogurt Dressing	70
156.	Avocado Cilantro Dressing	70

157. Spicy Dipping Sauce 70

158. Maple Shallot Vinaigrette 71

159. Pear and Poppy Jam 71

Smoothies **72**

160. Strawberry Smoothie 72

161. Cantaloupe Smoothie 72

162. Berry and Spinach Smoothie 72

163. Tropical Smoothie 72

164. Watermelon and Cantaloupe Smoothie 73

165. Green Detox Smoothie 73

166. Detox Smoothie 73

167. Banana Chocolate Smoothie 73

168. Green Tea Pineapple Smoothie 73

169. Banana Sorbet 74

Desserts **75**

170. Honeydew & Ginger Smoothies 75

171. Apple Cheesecake 75

172. Cherry and Chocolate Dessert 76

173. Frozen Citrus Cups 76

174. Chocolate Chip Fat Bomb 76

175. Pecan Clusters 77

176. Classic Fudge 77

177. Lemon Poppy Seed Cake 77

178. Chocolate Mug Cake 78

179. Cinnamon Roll Chilled 78

180. Toffee Apple Mini Pies 78

181. Sweet Tapioca Pudding 78

182. Blueberry Cupcakes 79

183. Cinnamon Pears 79

184. Saffron Rice Pudding 79

185. Vermicelli Pudding 80

186. Chocolate Mousse 80

187. Peach Cobbler 80

188. Apple Pear Crisp 81

Conversion Tables

Volume

Imperial	Metric	Imperial	Metric
1 tbsp	15ml	1 pint	570 ml
2 fl oz	55 ml	1 ¼ pints	725 ml
3 fl oz	75 ml	1 ¾ pints	1 liter
5 fl oz (¼ pint)	150 ml	2 pints	1.2 liters
10 fl oz (½ pint)	275 ml	2½ pints	1.5 liters
		4 pints	2.25 liters

Weight

Imperial	Metric	Imperial	Metric	Imperial	Metric
½ oz	10 g	4 oz	110 g	10 oz	275 g
¾ oz	20 g	4½ oz	125 g	12 oz	350 g
1 oz	25 g	5 oz	150 g	1 lb.	450 g
1½ oz	40 g	6 oz	175 g	1 lb. 8 oz	700 g
2 oz	50 g	7 oz	200 g	2 lb.	900 g
2½ oz	60 g	8 oz	225 g	3 lb.	1.35 kg
3 oz	75 g	9 oz	250 g		

Oven temperatures

Gas Mark	Fahrenheit	Celsius	Gas Mark	Fahrenheit	Celsius
1/4	225	110	4	350	180
1/2	250	130	5	375	190
1	275	140	6	400	200
2	300	150	7	425	220
3	325	170	8	450	230
			9	475	240

Metric cups conversion

Cups	Imperial	Metric
1 cup flour	5oz	150g
1 cup caster or granulated sugar	8oz	225g
1 cup soft brown sugar	6oz	175g
1 cup soft butter/margarine	8oz	225g
1 cup sultanas/raisins	7oz	200g
1 cup currants	5oz	150g
1 cup ground almonds	4oz	110g
1 cup oats	4oz	110g
1 cup golden syrup/honey	12oz	350g
1 cup uncooked rice	7oz	200g
1 cup grated cheese	4oz	110g
1 stick butter	4oz	110g
¼ cup liquid (water, milk, oil etc.)	4 tablespoons	60ml
½ cup liquid (water, milk, oil etc.)	¼ pint	125ml
1 cup liquid (water, milk, oil etc.)	½ pint	250ml

Breakfast

1. Breakfast Parfait

Preparation Time: 5 minutes   Servings: 2

Ingredients:

- 4 oz. unsweetened applesauce
- 6 oz. non-fat and sugar-free vanilla yogurt
- ¼ teaspoon pumpkin pie spice
- ¼ teaspoon honey
- 1 cup low-fat granola

Directions: Mix all ingredients (except the granola) in a bowl.
Layer the mixture with the granola in a cup.
Refrigerate before serving.

Nutrition: Calories: 286, Fat: 2.9g, Carbs: 56.8g, Sugar: 2.1g, Protein: 8.1g

2. French Toast Sticks

Preparation Time: 6 minutes   **Cooking Time: 10-15 minutes**
Servings: 4

Ingredients:

- 3 slices low-sodium whole-wheat bread, each cut into 4 strips
- 1 tablespoon unsalted butter, melted
- 1 egg
- 1 egg white
- 1 tablespoon 2% milk
- 1 cup sliced fresh strawberries
- 1 tablespoon freshly squeezed lemon juice

Directions: Place the bread strips on a plate and drizzle with the melted butter.
In a shallow bowl, beat the milk, egg, and egg white.
Dip the bread into the egg mixture and place on a wire rack to let the batter drip off.
Air fry half of the bread strips at 375° F for 5 minutes, turning the strips with tongs once during cooking, until golden brown. Repeat with the remaining strips.
In a bowl, mash lemon juice and the strawberries with a potato masher. Serve the strawberry sauce with the French toast sticks.

Nutrition: Calories: 144, Fat: 4.9g, Protein: 7.2g, Carbs: 18.1g, Sugar: 6.9g

3. Omelet with Cheeses and Tomato

Preparation Time: 10 minutes   **Cooking Time: 20 minutes**
Servings: 2

Ingredients:

- 3 eggs
- 50 g. Parmesan cheese
- 2 tbsp. heavy cream
- 1 tbsp. olive oil
- 1 tsp. oregano
- 1 tsp. nutmeg
- Salt and pepper to tast

For the covering:

- 3–4 stalks basil
- 1 tomato
- 100 g. Mozzarella cheese, grated

Directions: Mix the cream and eggs in a medium bowl.
Add the grated parmesan, nutmeg, pepper, oregano, and salt and stir everything.
Heat the oil in a pan. Add half of the egg and cream mixture to the pan.
Let the omelet set over medium heat, turn it, then remove it. Repeat with the last half of the egg mixture.
Cut the tomato into slices and place it on top of the omelets. Spread the mozzarella over the tomato.
Place the omelets on a baking sheet and cook at 175° F for 10 minutes.
Decorate the omelets with the basil leaves.

Nutrition Calories: 401, Carbs: 7.1g, Protein: 20.9g, Fat: 33g

4. Chia Seed With Nuts and Pomegranate

Preparation Time: 5 minutes   Servings: 3
Ingredients:
- 20 g. hazelnuts
- 20 g. walnuts
- 120 ml. almond milk
- 4 tbsp. chia seeds
- 4 tbsp. pomegranate seeds
- 1 tsp. agave syrup

Directions: Finely chop the nuts.
Mix the almond milk with the chia seeds. Allow everything to soak for 20 minutes.
Stir the mixture with the agave syrup.
Pour 2 tbsp. of each mixture into a dessert glass.
Layer the chopped nuts on top. Cover the nuts with 1 tbsp. of chia mass.
Sprinkle the pomegranate seeds on top and serve everything.

Nutrition Calories: 247, Carbs: 6.7g, Protein: 1.2g, Fat: 17.3g

5. Smoothie With Mango, Apple, Spinach, and Muesli

Preparation Time: 10 minutes   Servings: 1

Ingredients:
- 150 g. yogurt
- 30 g. apple
- 30 g. mango
- 30 g. low carb muesli
- 10 g. spinach
- 10 g. chia seeds

Directions: Soak the spinach leaves and allow them to drain.
Peel the mango and cut it into strips.
Cut the apple into pieces.
Put everything except the mango alongside the yogurt in a blender, and make a puree out of it.
Put the spinach smoothie in a bowl. Add muesli, chia seeds, and mango.

Nutrition Calories: 361, Carbs: 19.7g, Protein: 12.4g, Fat: 17g

6. Porridge With Walnuts

Preparation Time: 5 minutes   **Cooking Time: 10 minutes**
Servings: 1

Ingredients:
- 50 g. raspberries
- 50 g. blueberries
- 25 g. ground walnuts
- 20 g. flaxseed, crushed
- 10 g. oatmeal
- 200 ml. nut drink
- 1 tsp. agave syrup
- 1/2 tsp. cinnamon
- salt

Directions: Warm the nut drink in a saucepan. Add the flaxseed, walnuts, and oatmeal, stirring constantly.
Stir in the cinnamon and salt. Simmer, stirring for 8 minutes. Sweeten with agave syrup.
Put the porridge in a bowl.
Wash the berries and allow them to drain. Add them to the porridge and serve everything.

Nutrition Calories: 377, Carbs: 10.8g, Protein: 19g, Fat: 26.2g

7. Coconut Pancakes

Preparation Time: 5 minutes   **Cooking Time: 5 minutes**
Servings: 4

Ingredients:
- 1 cup coconut flour
- 2 tbsp. arrowroot powder
- 1 tsp.. baking powder
- 1 cup coconut milk
- 3 tbsp. coconut oil

Directions: In a medium container, mix all the dry ingredients. Add the coconut milk and 2 tbsp. of coconut oil, then mix properly.
In a skillet, melt the remaining 1 tsp. of coconut oil. Pour a ladleful of the batter into the skillet, then swirl the pan to spread the batter evenly into a smooth pancake. Cook it for 2 minutes on medium heat until it becomes firm.
Turn the pancake to the other side, then cook it for an additional 2 minutes until it turns golden brown.
Cook the remaining pancakes in the same process.

Nutrition Calories: 376.2, Fat: 14.7g, Carbs: 53.7g, Protein: 6.6g

8. Banana Barley Porridge

Preparation Time: 15 minutes
Servings: 2

Cooking Time: 5 minutes

Ingredients:
- 1 cup unsweetened coconut milk, divided
- 1 small banana, peeled and sliced
- 1/2 cup barley
- 3 drops liquid Stevia
- 1/4 cup coconuts, chopped

Directions: In a bowl, mix barley with half the coconut milk and Stevia.
Cover the blending bowl, then refrigerate for 6 hours.
In a saucepan, mix the mixture with the remaining coconut milk. Cook for 5 minutes on moderate heat.
Then top it with the chopped coconuts and, therefore, the banana slices.

Nutrition Calories: 158.7, Fat: 8.3g, Carbs: 19g, Protein: 4.1g

9. Apple Filled Swedish Pancake

Preparation Time: 25 minutes
Servings: 6

Cooking Time: 32 minutes

Ingredients:
- 2 apples, cored and sliced thin
- 3/4 cup egg substitute
- 1/2 cup fat-free milk
- 1/2 cup sugar-free caramel sauce
- 1 tbsp. reduced-calorie margarine
- 1/2 cup flour
- 1 1/2 tbsp. brown sugar substitute
- 2 tsp. water
- 1/4 tsp. cinnamon
- 1/8 tsp. cloves
- 1/8 tsp. salt
- Non-stick cooking spray

Directions: Heat oven to 400ºF.
Place margarine in an ovenproof skillet and place in oven until margarine is melted.
In a medium bowl, whisk together egg substitute, cloves, flour, cinnamon, milk, and salt until smooth.
Pour batter in hot skillet and bake for 25 minutes until puffed.
Spray a medium saucepan with cooking spray. Heat over medium heat.
Add apples, brown sugar, and water. Cook, stirring, until apples are tender and golden brown, about 6 minutes.
Pour the caramel sauce into a microwave-proof measuring glass and heat 45 seconds, or until warmed through.
Spoon apples into pancakes and drizzle with caramel. Cut into wedges.

Nutrition Calories: 191, Carbs: 24.9g, Protein: 5.9g, Fat: 2.3g, Sugar: 11.4g, Fiber: 2g

10. Blueberry Muffin Loaf

Preparation Time: 15 minutes
Servings: 12

Cooking Time: 40 minutes

Ingredients:
- 6 eggs beaten
- 1/2 cup almond milk, unsweetened
- 1/2 cup blueberries
- 1/2 cup cashew butter
- 1/2 cup almond flour
- 1/4 cup coconut oil
- 2 tsp. baking powder
- 1/2 tsp. salt
- Non-stick cooking spray

Directions: Heat oven to 350ºF. Line a loaf pan with parchment paper and spray with cooking spray.
In a small bowl, melt butter and oil together in the microwave for 30 seconds. Stir until well combined.
In a second bowl, stir together the dry ingredients. Add butter mixture and mix well.
In another bowl, whisk the almond milk and eggs together. Add to the flour mixture and stir well. Fold in blueberries. Pour into the prepared pan and bake for 40 minutes.

Nutrition Calories: 161, Carbs: 4.5g, Protein: 5.7g, Fat: 12.8g, Sugar: 0.9g, Fiber: 1g

11. Cheese Spinach Waffles

Preparation Time: 10 minutes
Servings: 4

Cooking Time: 20 minutes

Ingredients:
- 2 strips bacon, cooked and crumbled
- 2 eggs, lightly beaten
- 1/2 cup cauliflower, grated
- 1/2 cup frozen spinach, chopped (squeeze water out first)
- 1/2 cup low-fat Mozzarella cheese, grated
- 1/2 cup low-fat cheddar cheese, grated
- 1 tbsp. margarine, melted
- 1/4 cup reduced-fat Parmesan cheese, grated
- 1 tsp. onion powder
- 1 tsp. garlic powder
- Non-stick cooking spray

Directions: Thaw spinach and squeeze out as much as possible, place it in a large bowl.
Heat a waffle iron and spray with cooking spray.
Add the remaining ingredients to the spinach and mix well.
Pour small amounts on the waffle iron and cook like you would for regular waffles.

Nutrition Calories: 184, Carbs: 2.1g, Protein: 13.8g, Fat: 13g, Sugar: 1.1g

12. Potatoes, Chicken Sausage, and Egg

Preparation Time: 15 minutes
Servings: 6

Cooking Time: 10 hours and 10 minutes

Ingredients:
- Cooking spray
- 12 oz. chicken sausage links, sliced
- 1 onion, sliced into wedges
- 2 red sweet peppers, sliced into strips
- 1 ½ lb. potatoes, sliced into strips
- ¼ cup low-sodium chicken broth
- Black pepper to taste
- ½ teaspoon dried thyme, crushed
- 6 eggs
- ½ cup low-fat cheddar cheese, shredded

Directions: Spray oil on a heavy foil sheet. Put the sausage, sweet peppers, onion, and potatoes on the foil.
Drizzle top with the chicken broth. Season with the pepper and thyme. Fold to seal.
Place the packet inside a cooker. Cook on low setting for 10 hours.
Meanwhile, boil the egg until fully cooked. Serve eggs with the sausage mixture.

Nutrition: Calories 282, Fat 11.1g, Carbs 22.8g, Fiber 3g, Sugar 2.9g, Protein 21.4g

13. Apple & Cinnamon Pancake

Preparation Time: 15 minutes
Servings: 4

Cooking Time: 10 minutes

Ingredients:
- ¼ teaspoon ground cinnamon
- 1 ¾ cups Better Baking Mix
- 1 tablespoon oil
- 1 cup water
- 2 egg whites
- ½ cup sugar-free applesauce
- Cooking spray
- 1 cup plain yogurt
- Sugar substitute

Directions: Blend the cinnamon and the baking mix in a bowl.
Create a hole in the middle and add the oil, water, egg and applesauce. Mix well.
Spray a pan with oil. Place it on medium heat. Pour ¼ cup of the batter. Flip the pancake and cook until golden.
Serve with yogurt and sugar substitute.

Nutrition: Calories: 229, Fat: 5.4g, Carbs: 35.9g, Fiber: 4g, Sugar: 0.8g, Protein: 8.8g

14. Buckwheat Grouts Breakfast Bowl

Preparation Time: 5 minutes, plus overnight to soak
Servings: 4

Cooking Time: 10 minutes

Ingredients:
- 3 cups skim milk
- 1 cup buckwheat grouts
- ¼ cup chia seeds
- 2 teaspoons vanilla extract
- 1/2 teaspoon ground cinnamon
- Pinch salt
- 1 cup water
- 1/2 cup unsalted pistachios
- 2 cups sliced fresh strawberries
- ¼ cup cacao nibs (optional)

Directions: In a large bowl, stir together the milk, groats, chia seeds, vanilla, cinnamon, and salt. Cover and refrigerate overnight.
The next morning, transfer the soaked mixture to a medium pot and add the water. Bring to a boil over medium-high heat, reduce the heat to maintain a simmer, and cook for 10 minutes.
Transfer to bowls and serve, topped with the pistachios, strawberries, and cacao nibs (if using).

Nutrition: Calories: 338, Fat: 7.5g, Protein: 16.5g, Carbs: 50.5g, Sugar: 13.5g, Fiber: 10g

15. Cinnamon and Coconut Porridge

Preparation Time: 5 minutes
Servings: 4

Cooking Time: 5 minutes

Ingredients:
- 2 cups of water
- 1 cup 36% heavy cream
- 1/2 cup unsweetened dried coconut, shredded
- 2 tablespoons flaxseed meal
- 1 tablespoon butter
- 1 and 1/2 teaspoon stevia
- 1 teaspoon cinnamon
- Salt to taste
- Toppings as blueberries

Directions: Add the listed ingredients to a small pot, mix well.
Transfer pot to stove and place it over medium-low heat. Bring to mix to a slow boil. Stir well and remove the heat.
Divide the mix into equal servings and let them sit for 10 minutes.

Nutrition: Calories: 170.2, Fat: 15.3g, Carbs: 5.6g, Protein: 3.4g

16. Steel-Cut Oatmeal Bowl with Fruit and Nuts

Preparation Time: 5 minutes
Servings: 4

Cooking Time: 20 minutes

Ingredients:
- 1 cup steel-cut oats
- 2 cups almond milk
- ¾ cup water
- 1 teaspoon ground cinnamon
- ¼ teaspoon salt
- 1/2 cups chopped fresh fruit, (blueberries, strawberries, raspberries, or peaches)
- 1/2 cup chopped walnuts
- ¼ cup chia seeds

Directions: In a medium saucepan over medium-high heat, combine the cinnamon, almond milk, oats, water, and salt. Bring to a boil, reduce the heat to low, and simmer for 15 to 20 minutes, until the oats are softened and thickened.
Top each bowl with fresh fruit, walnuts, and chia seeds before serving.

Nutrition: Calories: 286.5, Fat: 10.4g, Protein: 11.3g, Carbs: 37.4g, Sugar: 6.7g, Fiber: 10g

17. Apple Dumplings

Preparation Time: 10 minutes
Servings: 8

Cooking Time: 45 minutes

Ingredients:
Dough:
- One tablespoon butter
- One cup whole-wheat flour
- Two tablespoons buckwheat flour
- Two tablespoons rolled oats
- Two tablespoons apple liquor

Apple filling:

- *Six large tart apples, thinly sliced*
- *Two tablespoons honey*
- *One teaspoon nutmeg*
- *Zest of one lemon*

Directions: Heat the oven to 350 F. In a food processor, combine the butter, flour, and oats. Pulse the mixture a few times until it seems like a perfect meal. Attach apple liquor and pulse until the mixture begins to form a ball a few more times. Remove the mixture from the food processor, firmly wrap it in plastic and chill for 2 hours. Mix in the apples, and nutmeg. Add zest of lemon. Set aside.

Roll out a 1/4-inch thick frozen dough with added flour. Split into circles of 8 inches. Using an eight-cup muffin tin and coat the muffin tin loosely with cooking spray.

Over each lightly sprayed cup, lay a circle of dough. Gently push the dough in. Add apple mixture to cover.

Fold over the sides and press to seal on top. Bake at 350 F for 30 minutes, until golden brown.

Nutrition: Calories: 176.4, Fat: 2.2g, Carbs: 35.4g, Fiber: 6g, Protein: 3.5g

18. Eggs and Ham

Preparation Time: 25 minutes
Servings: 4

Cooking Time: 15 minutes

Ingredients:

- *4 eggs*
- *10 ham slices*
- *4 tbsp. of scallions*
- *A pinch of black pepper*
- *A pinch of sweet paprika*
- *1 tbsp. of melted ghee*

Directions: Grease a muffin pan with melted ghee.

Divide ham slices each muffin mold to form your cups. In a bowl, mix eggs with scallions, pepper, and paprika and whisk well. Divide this mix on top of the ham, introduce your ham cups in the oven at 400 °F and bake for 15 minutes. Leave cups to cool down before dividing on plates and serving.

Nutrition: Calories: 249.2, Fat: 9.4g, Fiber: 3g, Carbs: 5.3g, Protein: 13.7g

19. Chocolate Pudding Pies

Preparation Time: 10 minutes
Servings: 6

Cooking Time: 45 minutes

Ingredients:

- *One package (three ounces) instant chocolate pudding*
- *Two cups skim milk*
- *Six tablespoons whipped topping*
- *Six graham cracker crusts, individual sizes (each three inches in diameter)*
- *Sprinkles, for garnish*

Directions: Add the pudding and the milk into a medium-sized dish. Whisk so it's mixed equally.

Cover and refrigerate for about five minutes, before the pudding thickens.

Into each graham cracker crust, spoon 1/3 cup of prepared pudding.

Cover each with a whipped icing of One tablespoon and garnish with sprinkles. Serve immediately.

Nutrition: Calories: 174.5, Fat: 4.8g, Carbs: 29.4g, Protein: 4.5g, Fiber: 0.5g

20. Walnut and Oat Granola

Preparation Time: 10 minutes
Servings: 16

Cooking Time: 30 minutes

Ingredients:

- *4 cups rolled oats*
- *1 cup walnut pieces*
- *½ cup pepitas*
- *¼ teaspoon salt*
- *1 teaspoon ground cinnamon*
- *1 teaspoon ground ginger*
- *½ cup coconut oil, melted*
- *½ cup unsweetened applesauce*
- *1 teaspoon vanilla extract*
- *½ cup dried cherries*

Directions: Preheat the oven to 350ºF. Line a baking sheet with parchment paper.

In a large bowl, toss the walnuts, cinnamon, oats, pepitas, salt, and ginger. In a large measuring cup, combine the coconut oil, applesauce, and vanilla. Pour over the dry mixture and mix well.

Transfer the mixture to the prepared baking sheet. Cook for 30 minutes, stirring. Remove from the oven and allow the granola completely cool. Break the granola into pieces, and mix in the dried cherries.

Transfer to an airtight container, and store at room temperature for up to 2 weeks.

Nutrittion: Calories: 223.9, Fat: 14.4g, Protein: 5.2g, Carbs: 19.6g, Fiber: 3.1g, Sugar: 4.5g

21. Coconut and Berry Oatmeal

Preparation Time: 10 minutes   **Cooking Time: 35 minutes**
Servings: 6

Ingredients:

- *2 cups rolled oats*
- *¼ cup shredded unsweetened coconut*
- *1 teaspoon baking powder*
- *½ teaspoon ground cinnamon*
- *¼ teaspoon sea salt*

- *2 cups skim milk*
- *¼ cup melted coconut oil, plus extra for greasing the baking dish*
- *1 egg*
- *1 teaspoon pure vanilla extract*

- *2 cups fresh blueberries*
- *1/8 cup chopped pecans, for garnish*
- *1 teaspoon chopped fresh mint leaves, for garnish*

Directions: Preheat the oven to 350ºF. Lightly oil a baking dish and set it aside.
In a medium bowl, stir together coconut, oats, baking powder, cinnamon, and salt.
In a small bowl, whisk together milk, oil, egg, and vanilla until well blended.
Layer half the dry ingredients in the baking dish, top with half the berries, then spoon the remaining half of the dry ingredients and the rest of the berries on top.
Pour the wet ingredients evenly into the baking dish. Tap it lightly on the counter to disperse the wet ingredients throughout. Bake the casserole, uncovered, until the oats are tender, about 35 minutes.
Serve immediately, topped with the pecans and mint.

Nutrition: Calories: 295.5, Fat: 16.7g, Protein: 9.8g, Carbs: 26.4g, Fiber: 4.1g, Sugar: 10.2g

22. Cottage Pancakes

Preparation Time: 10 minutes   **Cooking Time: 20 minutes**
Servings: 4

Ingredients:

- *2 cups low-fat cottage cheese*
- *4 egg whites*
- *2 eggs*

- *1 tablespoon pure vanilla extract*
- *1½ cups almond flour*

- *Nonstick cooking spray*

Directions: Place the cottage cheese, egg whites, eggs, and vanilla in a blender and pulse to combine.
Add the almond flour to the blender and blend until smooth.
Place a large nonstick skillet over medium heat and lightly coat it with cooking spray.
Spoon ¼ cup of batter per pancake, 4 at a time, into the skillet. Cook the pancakes until the bottoms are firm and golden, about 4 minutes.
Flip the pancakes over and cook the other side until they are cooked through, about 3 minutes.
Repeat with the remaining batter.
Serve with fresh fruit.

Nutrition: Calories: 344 .5, Fat: 21.7g, Protein: 29.7g, Carbs: 10.7g, Fiber: 4.1g, Sugar: 4.6g

23. Buckwheat Crêpes

Preparation Time: 20 minutes   **Cooking Time: 20 minutes**
Servings: 5

Ingredients:

- *1½ cups skim milk*
- *3 eggs*
- *1 teaspoon extra-virgin olive oil, plus more for the skillet*

- *1 cup buckwheat flour*
- *½ cup whole-wheat flour*
- *½ cup 2 percent plain Greek yogurt*

- *1 cup sliced strawberries*
- *1 cup blueberries*

Directions: In a large bowl, whisk together milk, eggs, and 1 teaspoon of oil until well combined.
Into a medium bowl, sift together the buckwheat and whole-wheat flours. Add the dry ingredients to the wet ingredients and whisk until well combined and very smooth.
Allow the batter to rest for at least 2 hours before cooking.

Place a large skillet or crêpe pan over medium-high heat and lightly coat the bottom with oil.
Pour about ¼ cup of batter into the skillet. Swirl the pan until the batter completely coats the bottom.
Cook the crêpe for about 1 minute, then flip it over. Cook the other side of the crêpe for another minute, until lightly browned. Transfer the cooked crêpe to a plate and cover with a clean dish towel to keep warm.
Repeat until the batter is used up; you should have about 10 crêpes.
Spoon 1 tablespoon of yogurt onto each crêpe and place two crêpes on each plate.
Top with berries and serve.

Nutrition: Calories: 329.5, Fat: 6.7g, Protein: 16.5g, Carbs: 53.5g, Fiber: 7.9g, Sugar: 10.5g

24. Banana Crêpe Cakes

Preparation Time: 5 minutes   **Cooking Time: 20 minutes**
Servings: 4

Ingredients:
- *Avocado oil cooking spray*
- *4 ounces (113 g) reduced-fat plain cream cheese, softened*
- *2 medium bananas*
- *4 large eggs*
- *1/2 teaspoon vanilla extract*
- *1/8 teaspoon salt*

Directions: Heat a large skillet over low heat. Coat the cooking surface with cooking spray, and allow the pan to heat for another 2 to 3 minutes.
Meanwhile, in a medium bowl, mash the cream cheese and bananas together with a fork until combined. The bananas can be a little chunky.
Add vanilla, eggs, and salt, and mix well.
For each cake, drop 2 tablespoons of the batter onto the warmed skillet and use the bottom of a large spoon or ladle to spread it thin. Let it cook for 7 to 9 minutes.
Flip the cake over and cook briefly, about 1 minute.

Nutrition: Calories: 175.8, Fat: 8.5g, Protein: 9.6g, Carbs: 14.6g, Fiber: 2.1g, Sugar: 7.6g

Snacks and Appetizers

25.Ham and Goat Cheese Omelet

Preparation Time: 10 minutes
Servings: 1

Cooking Time: 10 minutes

Ingredients:
- 1 slice of ham, chopped
- 4 egg whites
- 2 teaspoons of water
- 2 tablespoons onion, chopped
- 1 tablespoon parsley, minced
- What you will need from the store cupboard:
- 2 tablespoons green pepper, chopped
- 1/8 teaspoon pepper
- 2 tablespoons goat cheese, crumbled
- Cooking spray

Directions: Whisk together the water, pepper and egg whites in a bowl till everything blends well.
Stir in the green pepper, ham, and onion.
Now heat your skillet over medium heat after applying the cooking spray.
Pour in the egg white mix towards the edge. As it sets, push the cooked parts to the center. Allow the uncooked portions to flow underneath. Sprinkle the goat cheese to one side when there is no liquid egg.
Now fold your omelet into half. Sprinkle the parsley.

Nutrition: Calories: 142.8, Carbs: 4.7g, Fiber: 1 g, Sugar: 0.3g, Fat 3.8g, Protein 22.4g

26.Bacon and Mushroom Bite-Size Quiche

Preparation Time: 45 minutes
Servings: 1 quiche

Cooking Time: 20 minutes

Ingredients:
- Eight slices bacon
- Quarter pound fresh mushrooms, chopped
- One tablespoon butter
- One-third cup chopped green onion
- Two-third cup shredded swiss cheese
- For double-crust pie, use homemade or purchased
- Five eggs
- Two-third cup sour cream

Directions: Preheat oven to 375 degrees F.
Roll out the pastry dough 1/16-inch thick on a lightly floured board.
Cut out 42 circles using a 3-inch cutter; re-roll scraps as required.
Fit circles of thinly greased two-half-inch muffin pans into the bottoms
Meanwhile, until crisp, drain, fry the bacon slices, crumble or chop.
Chop the mushrooms and sauté until limp and liquid disappears in the butter.
Combine the bacon, green onion, mushrooms, and cheese. Divide the filling uniformly between the muffin cups.
Beat the eggs together in a big cup, apply the sour cream and whisk until smooth. Into each muffin cup, add about 1 tablespoon.
Bake for 20-25 minutes until puffed and light brown. Cool for 5 minutes in pans; lift out.

Nutrition: Calories: 92.8, Protein: 3.1g, Carbs: 3.4g, Fat: 5.8g

27.Rice Cakes with Fire Jelly

Preparation Time: 5 minutes

Servings: 4

Ingredients:
- One-third cup sugar-free apricot preserves
- two tablespoons minced fresh jalapeño chili pepper
- twelve eaches miniature salt-and-pepper rice cakes
- One-third cup fat-free cream cheese
- One tablespoon fresh rosemary, chopped

Directions: Mix sugar-free preserves and chili pepper in a small bowl. Then place rice cakes with cream cheese; use the preserve mixture for topping. Sprinkle with rosemary at the end.

Nutrition: Calories: 54.8, Protein: 3.9g, Carbs: 10.8g, Fat: 0.8 g

28.Pesto Cauliflower

Preparation Time: 10 minutes
Servings: 4

Cooking Time: 25 minutes

Ingredients:
- Four cups Cauliflower
- One-quarter cup pesto sauce
- One-quarter cup parmesan cheese
- Add salt and pepper to taste

Directions: Mix the pesto sauce and cauliflower in a mixing dish. Mix until the cauliflower is covered in pesto sauce.
Cauliflower to be spread uniformly on the baking sheet. To taste, apply salt and pepper and parmesan cheese to be used as a topping. Bake at 350 degrees for 25–30 minutes.

Nutrition: Calories: 98.5, Protein: 2.7g, Carbs: 4.4g, Fat: 8.4g

29.Roasted Italian Green Beans & Tomatoes

Preparation Time: 5 minutes
Servings: 4

Cooking Time: 15 minutes

Ingredients:
- Half pound fresh green beans, trimmed and halved
- Half pound tomatoes, trimmed
- One tablespoon olive oil
- One tablespoon Italian seasoning

Directions: Heat oven to 425 degrees F. Put green beans in a 15x10x1-inches baking pan. The baking pan should be coated with cooking spray. Then mix oil, Italian seasoning, and salt. Sprinkle it over beans and bake for 10 minutes.

Insert tomatoes into the pan. Beans should be roasted until they become crisp-tender, and tomatoes are softened by leaving them for an additional four to six minutes.

Nutrition: Calories: 52.6, Protein: 2.6g, Carbs: 12.4g, Fat: 0.1g

30. Baked Omelet Mix

Preparation Time: 10 minutes
Servings: 12

Cooking Time: 45 minutes

Ingredients:
- 12 eggs, whisked
- 8 ounces spinach, chopped
- 2 cups almond milk
- 12 ounces canned artichokes, chopped
- 2 garlic cloves, minced
- 5 ounces feta cheese, crumbled
- 1 tablespoon dill, chopped
- 1 teaspoon oregano, dried
- 1 teaspoon lemon pepper
- A pinch of salt
- 4 teaspoons olive oil

Directions: Heat up a pan with the oil over medium-high heat, add the garlic and the spinach and sauté for 3 minutes. In a baking dish, combine the eggs with the artichokes and the rest of the ingredients.

Add the spinach mix as well, toss a bit, bake the mix at 375 degrees F for 40 minutes, divide between plates and serve for breakfast.

Nutrition: Calories: 185.8, Fat: 12.4g, Carbs: 4.8g, Protein: 9.8g

31. Zucchini Mini Pizzas

Preparation Time: 20 minutes
Servings: 24

Cooking Time: 10 minutes

Ingredients:
- 1 zucchini, cut into ¼ inch slices diagonally
- ½ cup pepperoni, small slices
- 1 teaspoon basil, minced
- ½ cup onion, chopped
- 1 cup tomatoes
- What you will need from the store cupboard:
- 1/8 teaspoon pepper
- 1/8 teaspoon salt
- 3/4 cup mozzarella cheese, shredded
- 1/3 cup pizza sauce

Directions: Preheat your broiler. Keep the zucchini in 1 layer on your greased baking sheet.

Add the onion and tomatoes. Broil each side for 1 to 2 minutes till they become tender and crisp.

Now sprinkle pepper and salt. Top with cheese, pepperoni, and sauce.

Broil for a minute. The cheese should melt. Sprinkle basil on top.

Nutrition: Calories: 28.7, Carbs: 1g, Fiber: 0g, Sugar: 1g, Fat: 1.9g, Protein 2.2g

32. Marinated Mushroom Wraps

Preparation Time: 15 minutes

Servings: 2

Ingredients:
- 3 tablespoons soy sauce
- 3 tablespoons fresh lemon juice
- 1½ tablespoons toasted sesame oil
- 2 portobello mushroom caps, cut into 1/4-inch strips
- 1 ripe Hass avocado, pitted and peeled
- 2 (10-inch) whole-grain flour tortillas
- 2 cups fresh baby spinach leaves
- 1 medium red bell pepper, cut into ¼ inch strips
- 1 ripe tomato, chopped
- Salt and freshly ground black pepper

Directions: Preparing the Ingredients

In a medium bowl, combine the soy sauce, 2 tablespoons of the lemon juice, and the oil. Add the portobello strips, toss to combine, and marinate for 1 hour or overnight. Drain the mushrooms and set aside.

To assemble wraps, place 1 tortilla on a work surface and spread with some of the mashed avocado. In the lower third of each tortilla, arrange strips of the soaked mushrooms and some of the bell pepper strips.

Sprinkle with the tomato and salt and black pepper to taste. Roll up tightly and cut in half diagonally. Repeat with the remaining Ingredients and serve.

Nutrition: Calories: 314, Fat: 21.7g, Protein: 22.9g, Carbs: 7.3 g

33.Grilled Peaches

Preparation Time: 5 minutes   **Cooking Time: 10 minutes**
Servings: 6

Ingredients:
- 6 fresh peaches, ripe
- 1 tablespoon olive oil
- 6 tablespoons fat-free whipped topping

Directions: Lightly grease a grill pan and preheat it over medium heat.
Cut the peaches in half and remove the pits.
Brush the cut sides with olive oil or spritz with cooking spray.
Place the peaches cut-side down on the grill for 4 to 5 minutes.
Flip the peaches and cook for another 4 to 5 minutes until tender.
Spoon the peaches into bowls and serve with fat-free whipped topping.

Nutrition: Calories: 99.7, Fat: 2.1g, Carbs: 17.7g, Protein: 1.9g, Sugar: 15.4g, Fiber: 2.3g

34.Dark Chocolate Almond Yogurt Cups

Preparation Time: 10 minutes   **Servings: 6**

Ingredients:
- 3 cups plain nonfat Greek yogurt
- ½ teaspoon almond extract
- ¼ teaspoon liquid stevia extract (more to taste)
- 2 ounces 70% dark chocolate, chopped
- ½ cup slivered almonds

Directions: Whisk together the yogurt, almond extract, and liquid stevia in a medium bowl.
Spoon the yogurt into four dessert cups.
Sprinkle with chopped chocolate and slivered almonds.

Nutrition: Calories: 169.5, Fat: 7.2g, Carbs: 10.6g, Protein: 15.1g, Sugar: 7.7g, Fiber: 2.2g

35.Lemon Fat Bombs

Preparation Time: 15 minutes   **Servings: 10**

Ingredients:
- Coconut butter, full-fat: 3/4 cup
- Avocado oil: 1/4 cup
- Lemon juice: 3 tablespoons
- Zest of lemon: 1
- Coconut cream, full-fat: 1 tablespoon
- Erythritol sweetener: 1 tablespoon
- Vanilla extract, unsweetened: 1 teaspoon
- Salt: 1/8 teaspoon

Directions: Place all the ingredients for fat bombs in a blender and pulse until well combined.
Take a baking dish, line it with parchment sheet, then transfer the fat bomb mixture on the sheet and place the sheet into the freezer for 45 minutes until firm enough to shape into balls.
Remove the baking sheet from the freezer, roll the fat bomb mixture into ten balls, and arrange the fat bombs on the baking sheet in a single layer.
Return the baking sheet into the freezer, let chilled until hard and set, and then store in the freezer for up to 2 months. Serve when required.

Nutrition: Calories: 163.7, Fat: 16.1g, Protein: 1.8g, Carbs: 0.4g, Fiber: 3g

36. Tiramisu Shots

Preparation Time: 15 minutes
Servings: 4

Cooking Time: 10 Minutes

Ingredients:
- 1 pack silken tofu
- 1 oz. dark chocolate, finely chopped
- ¼ cup sugar substitute
- 1 teaspoon lemon juice
- ¼ cup brewed espresso
- Pinch salt
- 24 slices angel food cake
- Cocoa powder (unsweetened)

Directions: Add tofu, chocolate, Sugar substitute, lemon juice, espresso and salt in a food processor.
Pulse until smooth. Add angel food cake pieces into shot glasses.
Drizzle with the cocoa powder. Pour the tofu mixture on top.
Top with the remaining angel food cake pieces. Chill for 30 minutes and serve.

Nutrition: Calories: 74.5, Fat: 1.1g, Carbs: 11.5g, Protein: 3.4g

37. Choco Peppermint Cake

Preparation Time: 15 minutes
Servings: 4

Cooking Time: 10 minutes

Ingredients:
- Cooking spray
- 1/3 Cup oil
- 15 oz. package chocolate cake mix
- 3 eggs, beaten
- 1 cup water
- ¼ teaspoon peppermint extract

Directions: Spray slow cooker with oil.
Mix all the ingredients in a bowl.
Use an electric mixer on medium speed setting to mix ingredients for 2 minutes.
Pour mixture into the slow cooker. Cover the pot and cook on low for 3 hours.
Let cool before slicing and serving.

Nutrition: Calories: 184.7, Fat: 7.1g, Carbs: 26.5g, Protein 4.1g

38. Low-Carb Biscuits

Preparation Time: 10 minutes
Servings: 4 biscuits

Cooking Time: 15 minutes

Ingredients:
- ¼ cup plain Greek yogurt
- 1½ cups finely ground almond flour
- From the Cupboard:
- 2 tablespoons unsalted butter, melted
- Pinch salt

Directions: Preheat the oven to 375° F.
Combine the yogurt, butter, and salt in a bowl. Stir to mix well.
Fold the almond flour in the mixture. Keep stirring until a dough without lumps forms.
Divide the dough into 4 balls, then bash the balls into 1-inch biscuits with your hands.
Arrange the biscuits on a baking pan lined with parchment paper. Bake in the preheated oven for 14 minutes or until well browned. Remove the biscuits from the oven and serve warm.

Nutrition: Calories: 311.8, Fat: 27.1g, Protein: 10.7g, Carbs: 8.2g, Fiber: 5.1g, Sugar: 1.5g

39. Aromatic Toasted Pumpkin Seeds

Preparation Time: 5 minutes
Servings: 4

Cooking Time: 45 minutes

Ingredients:
- 1 cup pumpkin seeds
- 1 teaspoon cinnamon
From the Cupboard:
- 1 tablespoon canola oil
- 2 (0.04-ounce / 1-g) packets stevia
- ¼ teaspoon sea salt

Directions: Preheat the oven to 300°F.

Combine the pumpkin seeds with cinnamon, stevia, canola oil and salt in a bowl. Stir to mix well.
Pour the seeds in the single layer on a baking sheet, then arrange the sheet in the preheated oven.
Bake for 45 minutes or until well toasted and fragrant. Shake the sheet twice to bake the seeds evenly.
Serve immediately.

Nutrition: Calories: 201.8, Fat: 17.8g, Protein: 9.2g, Carbs: 4.8g, Fiber: 2.3g, Sugar: 0.2g

40. Apple Pita Pockets

Preparation Time: 10 minutes
Servings: 2

Cooking Time: 2 minutes

Ingredients:
- ½ apple, cored and chopped
- ½ teaspoon cinnamon
- ¼ cup almond butter
- 1 whole-wheat pita, halved

Directions: Combine the apple, cinnamon, and almond butter in a bowl. Stir to mix well.
Heat the pita in a nonstick skillet over medium heat until lightly browned on both sides.
Remove the pita from the skillet. Allow to cool for a few minutes. Spoon the mixture in the halved pita pockets, then serve.

Nutrition: Calories: 314.6, Fat: 20g, Protein: 8.6g, Carbs: 30.9g, Fiber: 7.2g, Sugar: 20.2g

41. Cinnamon Rolls

Preparation Time: 10 minutes
Servings: 10

Cooking Time: 20 minutes

Ingredients:
- 1 instant yeast packet
- 1 egg, large
- ¾ cups of whole milk
- 2-3/4 cups of flour
- 1 tablespoon ground cinnamon
- What you will need from the store cupboard:
- 4 tablespoons of butter, melted and unsalted
- ¾ teaspoon salt
- 2 tablespoons of maple syrup

Directions: First, prepare your dough. Warm the milk and whisk in the yeast.
Keep it aside so that the yeast becomes foamy.
Beat the remaining butter, egg, flour, and salt until everything combines well.
Include ¼ cup flour. Knead your dough for a minute.
Line your cooker with parchment paper.
Create the filling. Create small rectangles with your dough and apply butter on top.
Add cinnamon. Sprinkle butter on top.
Roll the dough up. Cut into small pieces. Cook covered.
Take out and then whisk in the milk and maple syrup for the icing. Drizzle some milk over your rolls.

Nutrition: Calories 239.7, Carbs 40.7g, Fat 6.8g, Protein 4.3g, Fiber 4g

42. Parsley Chicken Breast

Preparation Time: 10 minutes
Servings: 4

Cooking Time: 40 minutes

Ingredients
- 1 tablespoon dry parsley
- 1 tablespoon dry basil
- 4 chicken breast halves, boneless and skinless
- 1/2 teaspoon salt
- 1/2 teaspoon red pepper flakes, crushed
- 2 tomatoes, sliced

Directions: Preheat your oven to 350 degrees F.
Take a 9x13 inch baking dish and grease it up with cooking spray.
Sprinkle the parsley, and basil and spread the mixture over your baking dish.
Arrange the chicken breast halves over the dish and sprinkle garlic slices on top.
Take a small bowl and add the parsley, basil, salt, red pepper and mix well. Pour the mixture over the chicken breast. Top with tomato slices and cover, then bake for 25 minutes.
Remove the cover and bake for 15 minutes more.

Nutrition: Calories: 149.7, Fat: 3.6g, Carbs: 3.8g, Protein: 25.7g

43. Almond Coconut Biscotti

Preparation Time: 5 minutes
Servings: 16 (Serving size is 2 cookies)

Cooking Time: 50 minutes

Ingredients:
- 1 egg, room temperature
- 1 egg white, room temperature
- ½ cup margarine, melted
- What you'll need from store cupboard:
- 2 ½ cup flour
- 1 1/3 cup unsweetened coconut, grated
- ¾ cup almonds, sliced
- 2/3 cup Splenda
- 2 tsp baking powder
- 1 tsp vanilla
- ½ tsp salt

Directions: Heat oven to 350 degrees. Line a baking sheet with parchment paper.
In a large bowl, combine dry Ingredients.
In a separate mixing bowl, beat other Ingredients together. Add to dry Ingredients and mix until thoroughly combined.
Divide dough in half. Shape each half into a loaf measuring 8x2 ¾-inches. Place loaves on pan 3 inches apart.
Bake for 25 minutes. Cool on wire rack 10 minutes.
With a serrated knife, cut loaf diagonally into ½-inch slices. Place the cookies, cut side down, back on the pan and bake another 20 minutes, or until firm and nicely browned. Store in airtight container.

Nutrition: Calories 233.7, Carbs 12.4g, Protein 5.3g, Fat 17.5g, Sugar 8.7g, Fiber 3g

44. BLT Stuffed Cucumbers

Preparation Time: 15 minutes
Servings: 4

Cooking Time: 30 minutes

Ingredients:
- 3 slices bacon, cooked crisp and crumbled
- 1 large cucumber
- ½ cup lettuce, diced fine
- ½ cup baby spinach, diced fine
- ¼ cup tomato, diced fine
- What you'll need from store cupboard:
- 1 tbsp. + ½ tsp fat-free mayonnaise
- ¼ tsp black pepper
- 1/8 tsp salt

Directions: Peel the cucumber and slice in half lengthwise. Use a spoon to remove the seeds.
In a bowl, combine the remaining ingredients and stir well.
Spoon the bacon mixture into the cucumber halves. Cut into 2-inch pieces and serve.

Nutrition: Calories 94.5, Carbs 3.7g, Protein 6.4g, Fat 5.6g, Sugar 1.8g, Fiber 1g

45. Cheese Crisp Crackers

Preparation Time: 5 minutes
Servings: 4

Cooking Time: 10 minutes

Ingredients:
- 4 slices pepper Jack cheese, quartered
- 4 slices Colby Jack cheese, quartered
- 4 slices cheddar cheese, quartered

Directions: Heat the oven to 400°F. Line a cooking sheet with parchment paper.
Place cheese in a single layer on prepared pan and bake 10 minutes, or until cheese gets firm.
Transfer to paper towel line surface to absorb excess oil. Let cool, cheese will crisp up more as it cools.
Store in airtight container, or Ziploc bag. Serve with your favorite dip or salsa.

Nutrition: Calories 252.6, Carbs 0.9g, Protein 15.3g, Fat 19.7g, Sugar 0g, Fiber 0g

46. Chili Lime Tortilla Chips

Preparation Time: 5 minutes
Servings: 10

Cooking Time: 15 minutes

Ingredients:
- 12 6-inch corn tortillas, cut into 8 triangles
- 3 tbsp. lime juice
- What you'll need from store cupboard:
- 1 tsp cumin
- 1 tsp chili powder

Directions: Heat oven to 350 degrees.

Place tortilla in a single layer on a large baking sheet.

In a small bowl stir together spices.

Sprinkle half the lime juice over tortillas, followed by ½ the spice mixture. Bake 7 minutes.

Remove from oven and turn tortillas over. Sprinkle with remaining lime juice and spices. Bake another 8 minutes or until crisp, but not brown.

Nutrition: Calories 64.6, Carbs 13.5g, Protein 1.8g, Fat 0.9g, Sugar 0g, Fiber 2g

Poultry

47.Mustard Chicken

Preparation Time: 10 minutes
Servings: 4

Cooking Time: 40 minutes

Ingredients:
- 4 chicken breasts
- 1/2 cup chicken broth
- 3-4 tablespoons mustard
- 3 tablespoons olive oil
- 1 teaspoon paprika
- 1 teaspoon chili powder
- 1 teaspoon garlic powder

Directions: Take a small bowl and mix mustard, olive oil, paprika, chicken broth, garlic powder, chicken broth, and chili. Add the chicken breasts and marinate for 30 minutes.
Take a lined baking sheet and arrange the chicken. Bake for 35 minutes at 375° F.

Nutrition: Calories: 530.8, Fat: 22.5g, Carbs: 9.7g, Protein: 64g

48.Sticky Chicken

Preparation Time: 10 minutes
Servings: 6

Cooking Time: 40 minutes

Ingredients:
- Six chicken drumsticks
- Six chicken thighs
- Three tablespoons light soy sauce
- Lemon juice
- Six garlic cloves, finely chopped
- One tablespoon ginger, finely chopped
- Three tablespoons ground allspice
- One finely chopped green chili

Directions: Put the soy sauce, lemon juice, garlic, ginger, allspice, and chili into a large bowl. Mix well all the ingredients.
Cut the chicken and fill with marinade. Cover the chicken with a cling film and leave in the fridge overnight.
Heat the oven to 390 degrees F.

Put the chicken in a roasting tin. Sprinkle leftover marinade.
Roast the chicken in the oven for forty minutes and take out when it gets sticky and golden.

Nutrition: Calories: 261.5, Protein: 42.8g, Carbs 5g, Fat 6.1g

49.Stuffed Chicken Breasts

Preparation Time: 10 Minutes   **Cooking Time: 20 Minutes**
Servings: 4

Ingredients:
- Forty-five oz boneless, skinless chicken breast cut into halves
- Four water-packed canned artichoke hearts, minced
- One tablespoon crushed dried oregano, preferably Greek
- Salt (optional)
- Freshly ground pepper
- One tsp olive oil
- One cup fat-free unsalted canned chicken broth
- One-fourth cup plus half tablespoon fresh lemon juice
- Four slices of lemon
- Two tablespoons cornstarch
- Chopped parsley for garnish

Directions: Remove any obvious chicken fat, rinse it and pat it dry. Season the chicken with salt and pepper.
Place the halves with the flat side of a meat mallet between 2 pieces of plastic wrap and pound until the chicken is very thin and flat.
Mix the heart of the artichoke and oregano. Put equal amounts of the artichoke mixture into the middle of each pounded chicken breast. Just roll up with a toothpick or skewer, secure.
Heat the oil over low heat in a non-stick pan. On both ends, add chicken and brown equally. Pour on the lemon juice and broth.
Cover chicken with lemon slices, and boil (about 15 to 20 minutes) until chicken is cooked through.
Shift chicken, discarding toothpicks/skewers, to a tray. Keep warm.
Mix cornstarch with the remaining 1 1/2 tsp of lemon juice using a fork. Apply to a skillet and whisk until slightly thickened, over high fire.
Spoon the chicken with lemon sauce. Garnish with parsley and lemon slices.

Nutrition: Calories: 188.6, Protein: 25.5g, Carbs 5.3g, Fat 6.2g

50.Oven Parmesan Chicken

Preparation Time: 15 minutes   **Cooking Time: 1 hour 10 minutes**
Servings: 6

Ingredients:
- One clove crushed garlic
- One-quarter lb. butter, melted
- One cup dried bread crumbs
- One-third cup grated Parmesan cheese
- Two tablespoons chopped fresh parsley
- 1 tsp salt
- Pinch of ground black pepper
- Four lb. chicken, cut into pieces

Directions: Heat oven to 350 degrees F.
Mix the crushed garlic with the melted butter in a bowl or a dish. Combine together the bread crumbs, cheese, parsley, salt, and pepper in a bowl. Put chicken pieces into garlic butter. Then cover it with crumb mixture.
Put coated chicken pieces into a moderately greased 9x13 inch baking dish. Sprinkle remaining garlic butter.
Bake uncovered in the preheated oven for another one and a quarter of hours. Bake till chicken is cooked through, and juices become visible.

Nutrition: Calories: 586.5, Protein: 43.7g, Carbs: 13.1g, Fat: 36.9g

51.Chicken with Caper Sauce

Preparation Time: 20 minutes   **Cooking Time: 18 minutes**
Servings: 5

Ingredients:
For Chicken:
- 2 eggs
- Salt and ground black pepper, as required
- 1 cup dry breadcrumbs
- 2 tablespoons olive oil
- 1½ pounds skinless, boneless chicken breast halves, pounded
- into ¾-inch thickness and cut into pieces

For Capers Sauce:
- 3 tablespoons capers
- ½ cup dry white wine
- 3 tablespoons fresh lemon juice
- Salt and ground black pepper, as required
- 2 tablespoons fresh parsley, chopped

Directions: For chicken: in a shallow dish, add the eggs, salt and black pepper and beat until well combined.
In another shallow dish, place breadcrumbs.
Dip the chicken pieces in egg mixture then coat with the breadcrumbs evenly.
In a large skillet, heat the oil over medium heat and cook the chicken pieces for about 5 minutes per side.
Transfer the chicken pieces onto a paper towel-lined plate.
With a piece of the foil, cover the chicken pieces to keep them warm.
In the same skillet, add all the capers sauce ingredients (except parsley) and cook for about 2-3 minutes, stirring continuously. Stir in the parsley and remove from heat.
Serve the chicken pieces with the topping of capers sauce.

Nutrition: Calories: 351.6, Fat: 13.2g, Carbs: 16.1g, Sugar: 1.5g, Protein: 35.3g

52. Chicken Enchilada Spaghetti Squash

Preparation Time: 5 minutes
Servings: 4

Cooking Time: 40 minutes

Ingredients:
- 1 (3 lb./1.4 kg.) spaghetti squash, halved lengthwise and seeded
- 1 1/2 tsp. ground cumin, divided
- Avocado oil or cooking spray
- 4 (4 oz./113 g.) chicken breasts, boneless and skinless
- 1 large zucchini, diced
- 3/4 cup red enchilada sauce, canned
- 3/4 cup shredded Mozzarella cheese

Directions: Preheat the oven to 400ºF.
Season both halves of the squash with 1/2 tsp. of cumin, and place them cut-side down on a baking sheet; bake for 25 minutes.
Meanwhile, heat a large skillet over medium-low heat. When hot, spray the cooking surface with cooking spray and add the chicken breasts, zucchini, and 1 tsp. of cumin. Cook the chicken for 5 minutes per side. Stir the zucchini when you flip the chicken.
Transfer the zucchini to a bowl and set aside. Remove the chicken from the skillet, and let it rest for 10 minutes or until it's cool enough to handle. Shred or dice the cooked chicken.
Place the chicken and zucchini in a large bowl, and add the enchilada sauce.
Remove the squash from the oven, flip it over, and comb through it with a fork to make thin strands.
Scoop the chicken mixture on top of the squash halves and top with Mozzarella. Return the squash to the oven and broil for 2–5 minutes, or until the cheese is bubbly.

Nutrition: Calories: 330.2, Fat: 104g, Protein: 35.4g, Carbs: 26.4g, Fiber: 2g, Sugar: 3.2g

53. Creamy and Aromatic Chicken

Preparation Time: 15 minutes
Servings: 4

Cooking Time: 30 minutes

Ingredients:
- 4 (4 oz./113 g.) boneless, skinless chicken breasts
- Salt and freshly ground black pepper, to taste
- 1 tbsp. extra-virgin olive oil
- 1/2 sweet onion, chopped
- 2 tsp. fresh thyme, chopped
- 1 cup low-sodium chicken broth
- 1/4 cup heavy whipping cream
- 1 scallion, white and green parts, chopped

Directions: Preheat the oven to 375ºF.
Rub the chicken with salt and pepper.
Heat the olive oil in an ovenproof pan over medium-high heat until shimmering.
Put the chicken in the skillet and cook for 10 minutes or until well browned. Flip halfway through. Transfer onto a platter and set it aside.
Add the onion to the skillet and sauté for 3 minutes or until translucent. Add the thyme, the broth, and simmer for 6 minutes or until the liquid reduces in half. Mix in the cream, then put the chicken back to the skillet.

Arrange the skillet in the oven and bake for 10 minutes.
Remove the skillet from the oven and serve them with scallion.

Nutrition: Calories: 286.5, Fats: 13.9g, Protein: 34.5g, Carbs: 3.7g, Fiber: 1.0g, Sugar: 0.8g

54. Roasted Chicken With Root Vegetables

Preparation Time: 20 minutes
Servings: 6

Cooking Time: 41 minutes

Ingredients:
- 1 tsp. fresh rosemary, minced
- 1 tsp. fresh thyme, minced
- 1 tsp. salt
- 1 tsp. ground black pepper
- 2 tbsp. olive oil, divided
- 6 (6 oz./170 g.) chicken breast halves, boneless, skinless
- 2 medium fennel bulbs, chopped
- 4 medium carrots, peeled and chopped
- 3 medium radishes, peeled and chopped
- 3 tbsp. honey
- 1/2 cup white wine
- 2 cups chicken stock
- 3 bay leaves

Directions: Preheat the oven to 375ºF.
Mix the rosemary, thyme, salt, and black pepper in a small bowl.
Heat 1 tbsp. of olive oil in a non-stick skillet over medium-high heat until shimmering.
Rub the chicken breasts with half of the seasoning mixture.
Place the chicken in the skillet and cook for 6 minutes or until lightly browned on both sides. Remove the meat from the skillet and set it aside.
Mix the fennel bulbs, carrots, and radishes in a microwave-safe bowl, then sprinkle with the remaining seasoning mixture and drizzle with honey, white wine, and the remaining olive oil. Toss to combine well.
Cover the bowl and microwave the root vegetables for 10 minutes or until soft.
Arrange the root vegetables and chicken on a baking sheet, pour the chicken stock, and the honey mixture remains in the bowl. Top them with bay leaves.
Place the sheet in the preheated oven and roast for 25 minutes.
Remove the sheet from the oven and transfer the chicken and vegetables to a large plate. Discard the bay leaves, then allow to cool for a few minutes before serving.

Nutrition: Calories: 363.2, Fats: 9.8g, Protein: 42.3g, Carbs: 21.8g, Fiber: 3.8g, Sugar: 14.6g

55. Mu Shu Chicken

Preparation Time: 20 minutes
Servings: 6

Cooking Time: 6 hours

Ingredients:
- 1/2 cup hoisin sauce
- 2 tbsp. water
- 4 tsp. toasted sesame oil
- 1 tbsp. cornstarch
- 1 tbsp. reduced-sodium soy sauce
- 3 garlic cloves, minced
- 1 (16-oz.) pkg. (coleslaw mix) cabbage with carrots, shredded
- 1 cup carrots, coarsely shredded
- 12 oz. chicken thighs, skinless, boneless
- 6 (8-inch) whole wheat flour tortillas
- 1/4 cup green onions

Directions: Combine the hoisin sance, water, sesame oil, cornstarch, and soy sauce in a bowl.
In a slow cooker, combine shredded carrots and coleslaw mix.
Cut the chicken into 1/8-inch slices, then cut each slice in half lengthwise. Place the chicken on top of the cabbage mix. Drizzle with 1/4 cup of the hoisin mixture.
Heat tortillas according to package directions. Fill tortillas with chicken mixture.
Top with green onions and serve.

Nutrition: Calories: 268.7, Fat: 7.6g, Carbs: 33.2g, Protein: 16.3g

56. Country-Style Wedge Salad With Turkey

Preparation Time: 10 minutes   Servings: 4

Ingredients
- 1 head bibb or butterhead lettuce, quartered
- 1 recipe buttermilk-avocado dressing (see below)
- 2 cups cooked turkey breast, shredded
- 1 cup halved grape or cherry tomatoes
- 2 hard-cooked eggs, chopped
- 4 slices less-fat bacon, low-sodium, crisp-cooked, and crumbled
- 1/4 cup red onion, finely chopped
- Cracked black pepper to taste

Directions: Arrange a quarter of lettuce on each plate. Drizzle half of the dressing over wedges. Top with the turkey, eggs, and tomatoes. Drizzle with the remaining dressing. Sprinkle with onion, bacon, and pepper.

To make the buttermilk-avocado dressing: In a blender, combine 3/4 cup buttermilk, 1/2 avocado, 1 tbsp. of parsley, 1/4 tsp. each salt, onion powder, dry mustard, and black pepper, and 1 garlic clove, minced. Cover and blend until smooth.

Nutrition: Calories: 227.8, Fat: 8.6g, Carb: 7.6g, Protein: 29.3g

57. Balsamic Chicken

Preparation Time: 10 minutes   Cooking Time: 20 minutes
Servings: 6

Ingredients:
- 6 chicken breast halves, skinless and boneless
- 1 teaspoon garlic salt
- Ground black pepper
- 2 tablespoons olive oil
- 1 onion, thinly sliced
- 14 and 1/2 ounces tomatoes, diced
- 1/2 cup balsamic vinegar
- 1 teaspoon dried basil
- 1 teaspoon dried oregano
- 1 teaspoon dried rosemary
- 1/2 teaspoon dried thyme

Directions: Season both sides of your chicken breasts thoroughly with pepper, salt and garlic.
Take a skillet and place it over medium heat.
Add some oil and cook the seasoned chicken for 3-4 minutes per side until the breasts are browned.
Pour the diced up tomatoes and balsamic vinegar over the chicken, and season with rosemary, basil, thyme, and rosemary. Simmer the chicken for about 15 minutes until they are no longer pink.

Nutrition: Calories: 195.8, Fat: 6.7g, Carbs: 6.8g, Protein: 23.7g

58. Buffalo Chicken and Cheese Meatballs

Preparation Time: 5 minutes   Cooking Time: 20 minutes
Servings: 6

Ingredients:
- Chicken (ground) – 1 ½ pounds
- Egg whites – 2 medium
- Blue cheese – ½ cup
- Green onions (chopped) – ½ cup
- Buffalo sauce – ½ cup
- Olive oil – 1 tablespoon

Directions: Start by preheating the oven by setting the temperature to 400 degrees F.
Take a baking sheet and line it with parchment paper.
In a mixing bowl, add the egg whites, ground chicken, ¾ of buffalo sauce, and scallions. Mix well.
Take the blue cheese and crumble it well. Now add the crumbled cheese to the chicken mixture and fold it gently.
Use a large spoon to scoop out the mixture. Roll it into balls measuring about an inch. Place the prepared meatballs onto the lined baking sheet. Repeat the process with the remaining meat and cheese mixture.
Place the baking sheet into the preheated oven and bake for around 15 minutes.
Meanwhile, take a small bowl and add in the olive oil and buffalo sauce. Whisk well to combine.
Once the meatballs are done, transfer them onto a fresh sheet of parchment paper. Drizzle the meatballs with prepared buffalo sauce and olive oil mixture.
Return the meatballs to the oven and bake for another couple of minutes.

Nutrition: Fat: 14.5g, Protein: 23.4g, Carbs: 0.8g, Sugar: 0.9g

59. Turkey Scaloppini

Preparation Time: 10 minutes
Servings: 4

Cooking Time: 10 minutes

Ingredients:

- 1/2 cup whole-wheat flour
- 1/2 teaspoon sea salt
- 1/4 teaspoon freshly ground black pepper
- 3 tablespoons extra-virgin olive oil
- 12 ounces turkey breast, cut into 1/2-inch-thick cutlets and pounded flat (see headnote)
- 1 garlic clove, minced
- 1/2 cup dry white wine
- 2 tablespoons chopped fresh rosemary
- 1 cup low-sodium chicken broth
- 2 tablespoons salted butter, very cold, cut into small pieces

Directions: Preheat the oven to 200F. Line a baking sheet with parchment paper.

In a medium bowl, whip together the flour, salt, and pepper.

In a large skillet over medium-high heat, warmth the olive oil until it shimmers.

Working in batches with one or two pieces of turkey at a time, dredge the turkey cutlets in the flour and pat off any excess. Cook in the hot oil until the turkey is cooked through, about 3 minutes per side. Add more oil if needed.

Place the cooked cutlets on the lined baking sheet and keep them warm in the oven while you cook the remaining turkey and make the pan sauce.

Once all the turkey is cooked and warming in the oven, add the garlic to the pan and cook for 30 seconds, stirring constantly. Add the wine and use the side of a spoon to scrape any browned bits off the bottom of the pan. Simmer, stirring, for 1 minute. Add the rosemary and chicken broth. Simmer, stirring, until it thickens, 1 to 2 minutes more.

Whisk in the cold butter until incorporated. Return the turkey cutlets to the sauce and turn once to coat. Serve with any remaining sauce spooned over the top.

Nutrition: Calories: 343.8, Fat: 19.8g, Carbs: 14.6g, Fiber: 2g, Protein: 23.7g

60. Garlic Chicken

Preparation Time: 15 minutes
Servings: 4

Cooking Time: 40 minutes

Ingredients:

- Two ounces butter
- Two pounds chicken drumsticks
- Pepper
- Salt
- Lemon juice
- Two tbsps. Olive oil
- Seven cloves garlic
- Half cup parsley

Directions: Warm-up oven at 250°F.

Put the chicken in a baking dish. Add pepper and salt.

Add olive oil with lemon juice over the chicken. Sprinkle parsley and garlic on top.

Bake within forty minutes. Serve.

Nutrition: Calories: 539.8, Protein: 41.8g, Carbs: 2.8g, Fat: 38.1g, Fiber: 1.6g

Red Meat

61. Pepper Steak Stew

Preparation Time: 5 minutes
Servings: 6

Cooking Time: 2 hours

Ingredients:
- 1 lb. lean sirloin steak, slice into pieces
- Two coarsely chopped green peppers
- One diced medium onion
- Three large peeled and diced potatoes
- 3/4 cup of fat-free beef gravy
- A quarter tablespoon of dried minced garlic

Directions: Spray an ovenproof dish with oil for cooking.
Add steak, green peppers, onion, and potatoes and stir. Add gravy and garlic together.
Bake for about two hours in a 320°F oven.

Nutrition: Calories: 249.6, Protein: 27.9g, Carbs: 16.1g, Fat: 8.8g

62. Greek Lamb Salad

Preparation Time: 45 minutes
Servings: 4

Cooking Time: 5 minutes

Ingredients:
- Half cup low-fat natural yogurt
- Half tablespoon lemon juice
- One crushed garlic clove
- Half tablespoon ground cumin
- 1 lb. lamb loin chop, bones removed and fat trimmed
- Three tablespoons olive oil
- Two tablespoons fresh mint, shredded
- 3 oz. shredded lettuce
- Half chopped fresh cucumber
- Three tomatoes, sliced into thin wedges
- Half medium sliced red onion
- Half cup roughly chopped fresh coriander leaves
- Eight pieces of roasted wholegrain bread

Directions: Add the yogurt, lemon juice, garlic, and cumin to a tiny mixing bowl to create the dressing. Mix thoroughly.
In a ziploc bag, put one-third of the dressing, add the lamb, seal the bag and give it a shake to coat the lamb.
Marinate the meat in the fridge for a period of 30 minutes.
Save the remainder of the dressing for later in the refrigerator.
Add the olive oil in a non-stick pan over medium heat. Add the lamb and cook on either side for a couple of minutes.
Add more of the mint to the remainder of the dressing.

On each plate, place the salad (lettuce, tomato, cucumber, and onion). Sprinkle the remaining little bit of mint and the cilantro with it. Add the lamb to the salad and drizzle some of the sauce over the whole salad. Serve with two pieces of toast per dishes.

Nutrition: Calories: 130.5, Protein: 22.2g, Carbs: 8.1g, Fat: 11.7g

63. Braised Lamb with Carrots

Preparation Time: 25 minutes　　　　　　　　　　　**Cooking Time: 2 hours 10 minutes**
Servings: 4

Ingredients:
- One tablespoon coconut oil
- Two pounds lamb shoulder chops
- One sliced large onion
- Half cup mushrooms
- Three sliced cloves of garlic
- A quarter tablespoon allspice
- One tablespoon smoked paprika

- Three to five sprigs of fresh thyme
- Two to three branches of fresh rosemary
- Half tablespoon salt
- Two bay leaves
- Half tablespoon freshly ground black pepper

- One cup white wine
- Two cups chicken broth (no salt added)
- One to two cups beef broth
- Eight medium carrots (cut diagonally into 2") or mixed root vegetables
- One tablespoon Dijon mustard

Directions: Preheat the oven to 325 ° F.
Season the lamb with salt and pepper. Heat the coconut oil in a large saucepan over medium-high heat and brown the lamb on each side for about 1-2 minutes. Remove and set aside from the pot.
Add the mushrooms, onions, and garlic to the pot and cook until the onions start to soften for about 3 minutes. Stir in all the spices, paprika, bay leaves, salt and pepper, and add the wine. Add the chicken broth and carrots. Carry it to a boil and let it simmer for about three minutes.
Return the meat to the pot and lay the vegetables and sauce on top. Divide the mustard on top of each shoulder chop and spread it out. Cover with thyme and rosemary sprigs. Apply sufficient beef broth to coat the sides of the lamb with liquid. Cover and roast for 2 hours in the oven. Remove the meat and serve with the broth and the vegetables.

Nutrition: Calories: 300.8, Protein: 26.2g, Carbs: 18.1g, Fat: 10.2g, Sugar: 10.8g

64. Beef, Artichoke & Mushroom Stew

Preparation Time: 20 minutes　　　　　　　　　　**Cooking Time: 2 hours and 30 minutes**
Servings: 6

Ingredients:
For Beef Marinade:
- 1 onion, chopped
- 1 garlic clove, crushed
- 2 tablespoons fresh thyme, hopped

- ½ cup dry red wine
- 2 tablespoons tomato puree
- 2 tablespoons olive oil
- 1 teaspoon cayenne pepper

- Pinch of salt and ground black pepper
- 1½ pounds beef stew meat, cut into large chunks

For Stew:
- 2 tablespoons olive oil
- 2 tablespoons all-purpose flour
- ½ cup water
- ½ cup dry red wine

- 12 ounces jar artichoke hearts, drained and cut into small chunks

- 4 ounces button mushrooms, sliced
- Salt and ground black pepper, as required

Directions: For marinade: in a large bowl, add all the ingredients except the beef and mix well.
Add the beef and coat with the marinade generously. Refrigerate to marinate overnight.
Remove the beef from bowl, reserving the marinade.
In a large pan, heat the oil and sear the beef in 2 batches for about 5 minutes or until browned.
With a slotted spoon, transfer the beef into a bowl.
In the same pan, add the reserved marinade, flour, water and wine and stir to combine.
Stir in the cooked beef and bring to a boil.
Reduce the heat to low and simmer, covered for about 2 hours, stirring occasionally.
Stir in the artichoke hearts and mushrooms and simmer for about 30 minutes.
Stir in the salt and black pepper and bring to a boil over high heat.

Nutrition: Calories: 366.5, Fat 16.1g, Carbs: 9.2g, Sugar: 1.8g, Protein: 37.1g

65. Italian Beef

Preparation Time: 20 minutes
Servings: 4

Cooking Time: 1 hour 20 minutes

Ingredients:
- Cooking spray
- 2 lb. beef round steak, trimmed and sliced
- 1/2 cup onion, chopped
- 2 garlic cloves, minced
- 1 cup green bell pepper, chopped
- 1/2 cup celery, chopped
- 2 cups mushrooms, sliced
- 14 1/2 oz. tomatoes, canned and diced
- 1/2 tsp. basil, dried
- 1/4 tsp. oregano, dried
- 1/8 tsp. red pepper, crushed
- 2 tbsp. Parmesan cheese, grated

Directions: Spray the oil on the pan over medium heat.
Cook the meat until brown on both sides.
Transfer the meat to a plate.
Add the onion, garlic, bell pepper, celery, and mushroom to the pan; cook until tender.
Add the tomatoes, herbs, and pepper. Put the meat back in the pan.
Simmer while covered for 1 hour 15 minutes; stir occasionally.
Sprinkle Parmesan cheese on top of the dish before serving.

Nutrition: Calories: 211.7, Fat: 3.7g, Protein: 20.3g, Carbs: 1.7g, Fiber: 5g, Sugar: 5.4g

66. Skirt Steak With Peanut Sauce

Preparation Time: 10 minutes
Servings: 4

Cooking Time: 10 minutes

Ingredients:
- 1/3 cup light coconut milk
- 1 tsp. curry powder
- 1 tsp. coriander powder
- 1 tsp. reduced-sodium soy sauce
- 1 1/4 lb. skirt steak
- Cooking spray
- 1/2 cup Asian Peanut Sauce

Directions: Whisk together the coconut milk, coriander powder, curry powder, and soy sauce in a large bowl. Add the steak and turn to coat.
Cover the bowl and refrigerate for 30 minutes.
Preheat the barbecue with cooking spray and place the steak over medium-high heat.
Grill the steak for 3 minutes per side and let it rest for 5 minutes.
Slice the steak into 5 oz. pieces and serve with 2 tbsp. of the Peanut Sauce.

Nutrition: Calories: 360.6, Fat: 21.7g, Protein: 35.7g, Carbs: 7.7g, Fiber: 5g

67. Brisket With Cauliflower

Preparation Time: 5 minutes
Servings: 4

Cooking Time: 15 minutes

Ingredients:
- 1 cup water
- 2 cups, fresh cauliflower, chopped
- 3 tbsps. butter
- 1/4 onion, diced
- 1/4 cup pickled jalapeño slices
- 2 cups brisket, cooked
- 2 oz. cream cheese, softened
- 1 cup sharp cheddar cheese, shredded
- 1/4 cup heavy cream
- 1/4 cup crumbled bacon, cooked
- 2 tbsps. green onions, sliced

Directions: Add water to the instant pot.
Steam the cauliflower on a steamer basket for 1 minute.
Release pressure and set aside. Pour out water and press SAUTÉ.
Add jalapeño slices, butter, and onion.
Sauté for 4 minutes, add cooked brisket and cream cheese.
Cook 2 more minutes. Add heavy cream, cauliflower, and sharp cheddar.
Press CANCEL and mix until mixed well.
Sprinkle with green onions and crumbled bacon.

Nutrition: Calories: 573.7, Fats: 39.5g, Protein: 33.5g, Carbs: 7.5g

68. Butter Beef and Spinach

Preparation Time: 2 minutes
Servings: 4

Cooking Time: 10 minutes

Ingredients:
- 1 lb. 85% lean ground beef
- 1 cup water
- 4 cups fresh spinach
- 3/4 tsp. salt
- 1/4 cup butter
- 1/4 tsp. pepper
- 1/4 tsp. garlic powder

Directions: Brown the beef on SAUTÉ mode in the instant pot.
Remove it into a bowl. Drain the grease and clean the pot.
Add the water into the pot and place the steam rack.
Place the bowl with the beef on top.
Add the garlic powder, pepper, butter, salt, and spinach. Cover it with foil and close the lid.
Press MANUAL and cook 2 minutes on HIGH.
Make a quick release of pressure. Remove foil, stir and serve.

Nutrition: Calories: 271.7, Fats: 18.4g, Protein: 18.6g, Carbs: 0.9g

69. Low-fat Steak

Preparation Time: 25 minutes
Servings: 3

Cooking Time: 10 minutes

Ingredients:
- 400 g beef steak
- 1 tsp. white pepper
- 1 tsp. turmeric
- 1 tsp. cilantro
- 1 tsp. olive oil
- 3 tsp. lemon juice
- 1 tsp. oregano
- 1 tsp. salt
- 100 g water

Directions: Rub the steaks with white pepper and turmeric, and put them in the big bowl.
Sprinkle the meat with cilantro, oregano, salt, and lemon juice.
Leave the steak for 20 minutes.
Combine olive oil and water and pour it into the bowl with steaks.
Grill the steaks in the air fryer for 10 minutes from both sides.

Nutrition: Calories: 267.8, Protein: 41.1g, Fat: 9.7g, Carbs: 1.1g

70. Steak Sandwich

Preparation Time: 10 minutes
Servings: 4

Cooking Time: 10 minutes

Ingredients:
- 2 tablespoons balsamic vinegar
- 2 teaspoons freshly squeezed lemon juice
- 1 teaspoon fresh parsley, chopped
- 2 teaspoons fresh oregano, chopped
- 2 teaspoons garlic, minced
- 2 tablespoons olive oil
- 1 pound (454 g) flank steak, trimmed of fat
- 4 whole-wheat pitas
- 1 tomato, chopped
- 1 ounce (28 g) low-sodium feta cheese
- 2 cups lettuce, shredded
- 1 red onion, thinly sliced

Directions: Combine the lemon juice, balsamic vinegar, oregano, parsley, garlic, and olive oil in a bowl.
Dunk the steak to coat well, then wrap the bowl in plastic and refrigerate for at least 1 hour.
Preheat the oven to 450ºF.
Remove the bowl from the refrigerator. Discard the marinade and arrange the steak on a baking sheet lined with aluminum foil.
Broil in the preheated oven for 10 minutes for medium. Flip the steak halfway through the cooking time.
Remove the steak from the oven and allow to cool for 10 minutes. Slice the steak into strips.
Assemble the pitas with steak, tomato, feta cheese, lettuce, and onion to make the sandwich, and serve warm.

Nutrition: Calories: 344.7, Fat: 15.1g, Protein: 28.6g, Carbs: 22.2g, Fiber: 3.1g, Carbs: 18.2g

71. Coffeed and Herbed Steak

Preparation Time: 10 minutes
Servings: 4

Cooking Time: 10 minutes

Ingredients:
- ¼ cup whole coffee beans
- 2 teaspoons fresh rosemary, chopped
- 2 teaspoons fresh thyme, chopped
- 2 teaspoons garlic, minced
- 1 teaspoon freshly ground black pepper
- 2 tablespoons apple cider vinegar
- 2 tablespoons olive oil
- 1 pound (454 g) flank steak, trimmed of fat

Directions: Put the coffee beans, thyme, rosemary, garlic, and black pepper in a food processor. Pulse until well ground and combined.
Pour the mixture in a bowl, then pour the vinegar and olive oil in the bowl. Stir to mix well.
Dunk the steak in the mixture, then wrap the bowl in plastic and refrigerate to marinate for 2 hours.
Preheat the broiler to MEDIUM.
Remove the bowl from the refrigerator, and discard the marinade.
Place the marinated steak on a baking sheet lined with aluminum foil.
Broil in the preheated broiler for 10 minutes. Flip the steak halfway through the cooking time.

Nutrition: Calories: 315.4, Fat: 19.1g, Protein: 31.6g, Carbs: 0g, Fiber: 0g, Sugar: 0g

72. Roasted Beef with Shallot Sauce

Preparation Time: 10 minutes
Servings: 4

Cooking Time: 100 minutes

Ingredients:
- 1½ pounds (680 g) top rump beef roast
- Sea salt and freshly ground black pepper, to taste
- 3 teaspoons extra-virgin olive oil, divided
- 3 shallots, minced
- 2 teaspoons minced garlic
- 1 tablespoon green peppercorns
- 2 tablespoons dry sherry
- 2 tablespoons all-purpose flour
- 1 cup sodium-free beef broth

Directions: Heat the oven to 300ºF.
Season the roast with salt and pepper.
Place a large skillet over medium-high heat and add 2 teaspoons of olive oil.
Brown the beef on all sides, about 10 minutes in total, and transfer the roast to a baking dish.
Roast until desired doneness, about 1½ hours for medium.
When the roast has been in the oven for 1 hour, start the sauce.
In a medium saucepan over medium-high heat, sauté the shallots in the remaining 1 teaspoon of olive oil, about 4 minutes.
Stir in the garlic and peppercorns, and cook for another minute. Whisk in the sherry to deglaze the pan.
Whisk in the flour to form a thick paste, cooking for 1 minute and stirring constantly.
Pour in the beef broth and whisk until the sauce is thick and glossy, about 4 minutes. Season the sauce with salt and pepper. Serve the beef with a generous spoonful of sauce.

Nutrition: Calories: 330.5, Fat: 17.8g, Protein: 36.8g, Carbs: 3.1g, Fiber: 0g, Sugar: 1.0g

73. Open-Faced Pub-Style Bison Burgers

Preparation Time: 10 minutes
Servings: 4

Cooking Time: 15 minutes

Ingredients:
- 2 tablespoons extra-virgin olive oil
- 1 onion, thinly sliced
- 1 pound ground bison
- 1 teaspoon sea salt, divided
- 1 cup blue cheese crumbles
- 4 slices sourdough bread
- 1 garlic clove, halved
- Pub Sauce

Directions: In a large skillet over medium-high heat, heat the olive oil until it shimmers. Add the onion. Cook about 5 minutes.
Set the onion aside, and wipe out the skillet with a paper towel and return it to the stove at medium-high heat.
Season the bison with the salt and form it into 4 patties. Brown the patties in the hot skillet until they reach an internal temperature of 140°F, about 5 minutes per side.
Sprinkle the blue cheese over the tops of the burgers and remove the skillet from the heat.

Cover the skillet with a lid and allow the cheese to melt.

Meanwhile, toast the bread and then rub the garlic halves over the pieces of toast to flavor them.

To assemble, put a piece of toast on a plate. Top with onion slices, place a burger patty on top, and then spoon the sauce over the patty.

Nutrition: Calories: 389.6, Fat: 22.8g, Carbs: 21.9g, Fiber: 1g, Protein: 27.5g

74.Broccoli Beef Stir-Fry

Preparation Time: 15 minutes   **Cooking Time: 15 minutes**
Servings: 4

Ingredients:
- 2 tablespoons extra-virgin olive oil
- 1 pound sirloin steak, cut into 1/4-inch-thick strips
- 2 cups broccoli florets
- 1 garlic clove, minced
- 1 teaspoon peeled and grated fresh ginger
- 2 tablespoons reduced-sodium soy sauce
- 1/4 cup beef broth
- 1/2 teaspoon Chinese hot mustard
- Pinch red pepper flakes

Directions: In a large skillet over medium-high heat, heat the olive oil until shimmering.

Add the beef. Cook, stirring for 3 minutes.

With a slotted spoon, detach the beef from the oil and set it aside on a plate.

Add the broccoli to the oil. Cook, stirring, about 4 minutes. Add the ginger and garlic, and cook, stirring constantly, for 30 seconds.

Set the beef to the pan, along with any juices that have collected.

In a small bowl, whisk together the soy sauce, broth, mustard, and red pepper flakes.

Attach the soy sauce mixture to the skillet and cook, stirring, until everything warms through, about 3 minutes.

Nutrition: Calories: 226.5, Fat: 10.6g, Carbs: 4.8g, Fiber: 1g, Protein: 27.7g

75.Slow-Cooker Roast with Green Beans

Preparation Time: 10 minutes   **Cooking Time: 8 Hours and 30 minutes**
Servings: 8

Ingredients:
- 2 medium stalks celery, sliced
- 1 medium yellow onion, chopped
- 1 (3-pound) boneless beef chuck roast
- Salt and pepper
- 1/4 cup beef broth
- 2 tablespoons Worcestershire sauce
- 4 cups green beans, trimmed
- 2 tablespoons cold butter, chopped

Directions: In a slow-cooking dish, add the celery and onion.

Put the frying pan on top and season with salt and pepper.

Whisk the beef broth and Worcestershire sauce together then pour in.

Cover and cook for 8 hours on low heat, until the beef is very tender.

Cut the beef into chunks.

Return the beef to the slow cooker and add the chopped butter and the beans.

Cover and cook for 20 to 30 minutes on warm, until the beans are tender.

Nutrition: Calories: 374.8, Fat: 13.1g, Protein: 52.4g, Carbs: 5.7g, Fiber: 2g

76.Baked Macaroni with Red Sauce

Preparation Time: 10 minutes   **Cooking Time: 45 minutes**
Servings: 6

Ingredients
- Half pound extra-lean ground beef
- One small onion, diced (about half cup)
- Seven oz. whole-wheat elbow macaroni
- Fifteen oz. reduced-sodium spaghetti sauce
- Six tablespoons Parmesan cheese

Directions: Heat the oven to 350 F. Coat a baking dish lightly with cooking spray.

Heat the ground beef and onion in a nonstick frying pan until the meat is browned. Drain and put aside.

Fill 3/4 of a large pot full of water and bring it to a boil. Add the pasta and cook according to the product directions. Thoroughly drain the pasta.

Add the cooked pasta and spaghetti sauce to the meat and onions. Stir to combine uniformly.

In the prepared baking dish, spoon the mixture into it and bake for about 25 minutes until bubbly.

Separate the macaroni into individual dishes. Sprinkle one tablespoon of Parmesan cheese for each one. Serve.

Nutrition: Carbs: 31.1g, Calories: 268.7, Protein: 15.5g, Fat: 8.7g, Fiber: 4g

Vegetables and Salads

77. Spinach Rolls

Preparation Time: 10 minutes
Servings: 2

Cooking Time: 40 minutes

Ingredients:
- Sixteen ounces frozen spinach leaves
- Three eggs
- Two and a half lb. onion
- Two ounces carrot
- One-ounce low-fat mozzarella cheese
- Four ounces fat-free cottage cheese
- Three quarter cup parsley
- One cloves garlic
- One tablespoon curry powder
- One fourth tablespoon chili flakes
- One tablespoon salt
- One tablespoon pepper
- Cooking spray

Directions: Preheat the oven to 400 ° F.
Thaw the spinach and drain the water with a strainer.
In a mixing bowl, mix the mozzarella, 2 eggs, spinach, garlic, half the salt, and pepper.
Spray a baking sheet with cooking spray. Move the spinach mixture onto the sheet and push it down, about ½ inch thick and about 10 inches high. Bake for 15 minutes and then set aside on a rack to cool. Don't turn the oven off.
Chop the onion and parsley finely. Grate the carrots.
Fry the onions for a minute in a skillet with a little oil. Then add to the pan the carrots and parsley and let it boil for 2 min.
Add cottage cheese, chili, curry, the other half of the salt, and pepper. Briefly mix.
Take the fire off the pan, put an egg, and blend it all together.
Spread the filling over the spinach that has been cooled. Roll the spinach mat carefully, then bake for 25 minutes.
Take out the roll once the time is up and let it cool for 5-10 minutes before cutting it into slices and serving.

Nutrition: Calories: 307.5, Protein: 26.6g, Carbs: 18.1g, Fat: 9.2g, Sugar: 5.3g

78. Swiss Chard with Raisins & Pine Nuts

Preparation Time: 15 minutes
Servings: 4

Cooking Time: 20 minutes

Ingredients:
- Two pounds Swiss chard, stemmed (the stems diced)
- Vegetable broth
- Two minced garlic cloves
- Three tablespoons of raisins
- Three tablespoons of pine nuts
- Salt and ground black pepper

Directions: Put the raisins in a bowl and cover them with hot water. Soak for 10 minutes and rinse.
Fill a cup of ice water.
Over low heat, place a large pot of water on the stove and incorporate the chard. Cook for 2-3 minutes. Then move the chard to the ice water bowl and leave to rest for a minute. As much water as practicable, rinse and strain out and coarsely chop.
In a large pan, boil 1/2 cup of vegetable broth. Add the chard stems and cook until soft, about 3 to 5 minutes. Add the pine nuts and cook for another minute, stirring. Add the garlic and simmer for an extra minute or two. If it sticks, add more vegetable broth.
Mix together the sliced vegetables and raisins. With a little salt and ground black pepper, season to taste, and eat.

Nutrition: Calories: 150.7, Protein: 5.6g, Carbs: 14.9g, Fat: 9.8g

79. Diced Vegetable Salad

Preparation Time: 15 minutes

Servings: 8

Ingredients:
- Two diced small zucchinis
- Half cucumber, diced
- One diced red bell pepper
- One diced green bell pepper
- One diced yellow bell pepper
- Half diced red onion
- One diced hot house tomato
- One cup of cooked chickpeas
- Half cup roughly chopped parsley
- One cup crumbled feta cheese

For dressing:
- One minced clove garlic
- Half tablespoon kosher salt
- One tablespoon freshly ground black pepper
- One tablespoon dried oregano
- Half cup olive oil
- Three tablespoons red wine vinegar

Directions: Mix all vegetables in a big bowl with the cheese.
In another bowl, whisk the remaining ingredients together to create the dressing.
Pour the salad over the dressing and blend softly to absorb it.

Nutrition: Calories: 60.8, Fat: 3.1g, Carbs: 7.8g, Protein: 1.2g, Sugar: 2.8g

80. Broccoli and Bacon Salad

Preparation Time: 10 minutes   **Servings: 4**

Ingredients:
- 2 cups broccoli, separated into florets
- 4 slices bacon, chopped and cooked crisp
- 1/2 cup cheddar cheese, cubed
- 1/4 cup low-fat Greek yogurt
- 1/8 cup red onion, diced fine
- 1/8 cup almonds, sliced
- 1/4 cup reduced-fat mayonnaise
- 1 tbsp. lemon juice
- 1 tbsp. apple cider vinegar
- 1 tbsp. granulated sugar substitute
- 1/4 tsp. salt
- 1/4 tsp. pepper

Directions: In a large bowl, combine the cheese, broccoli, onion, bacon, and almonds.
In a small bowl, whisk the remaining ingredients together until combined.
Pour the dressing over the broccoli mixture and stir. Cover and chill at least 1 hour before serving.

Nutrition: Calories: 216.4, Carbs: 11.7g, Protein: 11.7g, Fat: 13.2g, Sugar: 5.7g, Fiber: 2g

81. Chopped Veggie Salad

Preparation Time: 15 minutes   **Servings: 4**

Ingredients:
- 1 cucumber, chopped
- 1 pint cherry tomatoes, cut in half
- 3 radishes, chopped
- 1 yellow bell pepper chopped
- 1/2 cup fresh parsley, chopped
- 3 tbsp. lemon juice
- 1 tbsp. olive oil
- Salt to taste

Directions: Place all the ingredients in a large bowl and toss to combine.
Serve immediately, or cover and chill until ready to serve.

Nutrition: Calories: 69.5, Carbs: 8.7g, Protein: 2.4g, Fat: 3.1g, Sugar: 4.7g, Fiber: 2g

82. Harvest Salad

Preparation Time: 15 minutes   **Cooking Time: 25 minutes**
Servings: 6

Ingredients:
- 10 oz. kale, deboned and chopped
- 1 1/2 cup blackberries
- 1/2 butternut squash, cubed
- 1/4 cup goat cheese, crumbled

Maple Mustard Salad Dressing:
- 1 cup raw pecans
- 1/3 cup raw pumpkin seeds
- 1/4 cup cranberries, dried
- 3 1/2 tbsp. olive oil
- 1 1/2 tbsp. sugar-free maple syrup
- 3/8 tsp. salt, divided
- Pepper, to taste
- Non-stick cooking spray

Directions: Heat oven to 400°F. Spray a baking sheet with cooking spray.
Spread the squash on the prepared pan, add 1 1/2 tbsp. of oil, 1/8 tsp. of salt, and pepper to squash and stir to coat the squash evenly. Bake for 20 minutes.
Place the kale in a large bowl. Add 2 tbsp. of oil and 1/2 tsp. of salt and massage it into the kale for 4 minutes. Spray a clean baking sheet with cooking spray.
In a medium bowl, stir together pumpkin seeds, pecans, and maple syrup until the nuts are coated. Pour onto a prepared pan and bake 8 minutes; these can be baked simultaneously as the squash.
To assemble the salad: Place all of the ingredients in a large bowl. Pour dressing over and toss to coat.

Nutrition: Calories: 435.4, Carbs: 23.2g, Protein: 9.4g, Fat: 36.2g, Sugar: 4.3g, Fiber: 7g

83. Layered Salad

Preparation Time: 10 minutes   **Servings: 10**

Ingredients:
- 6 slices bacon, chopped and cooked crisp
- 2 tomatoes, diced
- 2 stalks celery, sliced
- 1 head romaine lettuce, diced
- 1 red bell pepper, diced
- 1 cup frozen peas, thawed
- 1 cup sharp cheddar cheese, grated
- 1/4 cup red onion, diced fine
- 1 cup fat-free ranch dressing

Direction: Use a 9x13-inch glass baking dish and layer half the lettuce, pepper, celery, tomatoes, peas, onion, cheese, bacon, and dressing. Repeat. Cover and let cool until ready to serve.

Nutrition: Calories: 129.5, Carbs: 13.5g, Protein: 6.4g, Fat: 5.6g, Sugar: 4.9g, Fiber: 2g

84. Pickled Cucumber and Onion Salad

Preparation Time: 10 minutes   **Servings: 2**

Ingredients
- 1/2 cucumber, peeled and sliced
- 1/4 cup red onion, sliced thin
- 1 tbsp. olive oil
- 1 tbsp. white vinegar
- 1 tsp. dill

Directions: Place all the ingredients in a medium bowl and toss to combine.

Nutrition: Calories: 78.7, Carbs: 3.4g, Protein: 1.5g, Fat: 6.8g, Sugar: 1.6g, Fiber: 1g

85. Pomegranate and Brussels Sprouts Salad

Preparation Time: 10 minutes   **Servings: 6**

Ingredients:
- 3 slices bacon, cooked crisp and crumbled
- 3 cup Brussels sprouts, shredded
- 3 cup kale, shredded
- 1 1/2 cup pomegranate seeds
- 1/2 cup almonds, toasted and chopped
- 1/4 cup reduced-fat parmesan cheese, grated
- ½ cup Citrus Vinaigrette

Directions: Combine all the ingredients in a large bowl.
Drizzle the vinaigrette over salad, and toss to coat well.

Nutrition: Calories: 255.7, Carbs: 14.8g, Protein: 9.3g, Fat: 17.5g, Sugar: 4.2g, Fiber: 5g

86. Eggplant Surprise

Preparation Time: 10-20 minutes   **Cooking Time: 7 minutes**
Servings: 4

Ingredients:
- 1 eggplant, roughly chopped
- 3 zucchinis, roughly chopped
- 3 tbsp. of extra virgin olive oil
- 3 tomatoes, sliced
- 2 tbsp. of lemon juice
- 1 tsp. of thyme; dried
- 1 tsp. of oregano; dried
- Salt and black pepper to the taste

Directions: Put eggplant pieces in your instant pot. Add zucchinis and tomatoes.
In a bowl, mix lemon juice with thyme, salt, pepper, oregano and oil and stir well.
Pour this over veggies, toss to coat, seal the instant pot lid and cook at high for 7 minutes.
Quick-release the pressure, carefully open the lid; divide among plates and serve.

Nutrition: Calories: 159.7, Fat: 6.5g, Protein: 1.2g, Sugar: 5.8g, Carbs: 18.4g, Fiber: 8g

87. Pumpkin Custard

Preparation Time: 5 minutes   **Cooking Time: 2 hours 40 minutes**
Servings: 6

Ingredients:
- Eggs – 4 large
- Stevia erythritol blend (granulated) – ½ cup
- Pumpkin puree – 1 cup
- Vanilla extract – 1 teaspoon
- Almond flour (superfine) – ½ cup
- Pumpkin pie spice – 1 teaspoon
- Sea salt – 1/8 teaspoon
- Butter (melted) – 4 tablespoons

Directions: Start by greasing a 3-quart slow-cooker with coconut oil spray. Set aside.
Take a medium-sized glass mixing bowl and crack the eggs into the same. Use an electric mixer to whisk the eggs until smooth and frothy.
Gradually add in the sweetener and continue beating. Also, add in the pumpkin puree and vanilla extract, and mix until well combined.
In another bowl, sift in the pumpkin spice, almond flour, and salt. Transfer the ingredients to the egg mixture.
Add the melted butter in a stream while mixing continuously. Once done, transfer the mixture to the greased slow cooker.
Cover the cooker with a lid, turn the slow cooker to low and cook for around 2 hours 45 minutes.
Once done, transfer into a pudding cup and serve with whipped cream and a pinch of nutmeg powder.

Nutrition: Calories: 396, Fat: 14.8g, Protein: 7.5g, Carbs: 4.6g, Sugar: 1.8g

88. Mushroom and Cauliflower Risotto

Preparation Time: 10 minutes   **Cooking Time: 25 minutes**
Servings: 6

Ingredients:
- Butter – 2 tablespoons
- Onion (finely diced) – ½ large
- Portobello mushrooms (thinly sliced) – 1 pound
- Garlic (minced) – 2 cloves
- Fresh thyme – 1 teaspoon
- Cauliflower (riced) – 4 cups
- Chicken bone broth – ½ cup
- Heavy cream – ¾ cup
- Parmesan cheese (grated) – 1/3 cup
- Sea salt – ¾ teaspoon
- Black pepper – ¼ teaspoon
- Fresh cilantro (finely chopped) – for garnish

Directions: Begin by placing a nonstick saucepan over a medium flame. Add in the butter and let it melt.
Once the butter heats, add in the onions and mushrooms. Sauté until the mushrooms are slightly browned and tender, for about 15 minutes.
Stir in the thyme and garlic; sauté for around 1 minute.
Increase the heat to high and add cauliflower and the bone broth. Stir well. Bring the broth to a simmer.
Once the broth simmers, reduce the heat to medium-low and cook for about 5 minutes.
Reduce the heat to low and stir in the parmesan cheese and cream. Cook for another minute.
Season the risotto with black pepper and sea salt.
Transfer into a serving bowl and garnish with freshly chopped cilantro.

Nutrition: Calories: 211, Fat: 15.2g, Protein: 6.2g, Carbs 7.5g, Sugar 3.7g

89. Peppers with Sriracha Mayo

Preparation Time: 20 minutes   **Cooking Time: 10 minutes**
Servings: 2

Ingredients:
- 4 bell peppers, seeded and sliced (1-inch pieces
- 1 onion, sliced (1-inch pieces
- 1 tablespoon of olive oil
- 1/2 teaspoon of dried rosemary
- 1/2 teaspoon of dried basil
- Kosher salt, to taste
- 1/4 teaspoon of ground black pepper
- 1/3 cup of mayonnaise
- 1/3 teaspoon of Sriracha

Directions: Toss the bell peppers and onions with the olive oil, rosemary, basil, salt, and black pepper.
Place the peppers and onions on an even layer in the cooking basket. Cook at 400°F for 12 to 14 minutes.
Meanwhile, make the sauce by whisking the mayonnaise and Sriracha. Serve immediately.

Nutrition: Calories: 345.7, Fat: 33.7g, Carbs: 8.8g, Protein: 2.6g, Sugar: 4.1g

90. Spinach Rich Ballet

Preparation Time: 5 minutes
Servings: 4

Cooking Time: 30 minutes

Ingredients:
- 1½ lbs. Baby spinach
- 8 teaspoons coconut cream
- 14 oz. Cauliflower
- 2 tablespoons unsalted butter
- Salt
- Ground black pepper

Directions: Warm-up oven at 360 degrees F.
Melt butter, then toss in spinach to sauté for 3 minutes.
Divide the spinach into four ramekins.
Divide cauliflower, cream, salt, and black pepper in the ramekins. Bake within 25 minutes.

Nutrition: Calories 187.4, Fat 12.1g, Carbs 4.2g, Protein 15.1g

91. Quinoa and Lush Vegetable Bowl

Preparation Time: 15 minutes
Servings: 6

Cooking Time: 15 minutes

Ingredients:
- 2 cups vegetable broth
- 1 cup quinoa, well rinsed and drained
- 1 teaspoon extra-virgin olive oil
- ½ sweet onion, chopped
- 2 teaspoons minced garlic
- ½ large green zucchini, halved lengthwise and cut into half disks
- 1 red bell pepper, seeded and cut into thin strips
- 1 cup fresh or frozen corn kernels
- 1 teaspoon chopped fresh basil
- Sea salt and ground black pepper, to taste

Directions: Place a medium saucepan over medium heat and add the vegetable broth. Bring the broth to a boil and add the quinoa. Cover and reduce the heat to low.
Cook until the quinoa has absorbed all the broth, about 15 minutes. Remove from the heat and let it cool slightly.
While the quinoa is cooking, place a large skillet over medium-high heat and add the oil.
Sauté the onion and garlic until softened and translucent, about 3 minutes.
Add the zucchini, bell pepper, and corn, and sauté until the vegetables are tender-crisp, about 5 minutes.
Remove the skillet from the heat. Add the cooked quinoa and the basil to the skillet, stirring to combine. Season with salt and pepper, and serve.

Nutrition: Calories: 158.7, Fat: 2.8g, Protein: 7.7g, Carbs: 25.7g, Fiber: 2.9g, Sugar: 3.0g

92. Avocado White Bean Sandwich

Preparation Time: 5 minutes
Servings: 8

Cooking Time: 15 minutes

Ingredients:
- 2 medium avocado, pitted and chopped
- 1 (15-ounce) can white beans, rinsed and drained
- 2 tablespoons fresh lemon juice
- 1 tablespoon olive oil
- 1 to 2 cloves minced garlic
- Salt and pepper
- 8 slices whole-wheat or whole-grain bread
- 4 slices low-fat cheddar cheese
- 4 leaves romaine lettuce, halved

Directions: Combine the avocado, white beans, lemon juice, olive oil, and garlic in a medium bowl.
Mash the ingredients together then season with salt and pepper to taste.
Toast the slices of bread to your liking.
Spread the avocado white bean mixture on the slices of toast.
Top each with a half slice of cheese and a lettuce leaf to serve.

Nutrition: Calories: 124.8, Fat: 3.1g, Carbs: 16.8g, Protein: 6.7g, Sugar 7.2g, Fiber 3.6g

Pork Recipes

93.Jamaican Pork Tenderloin

Preparation Time: 10 minutes
Servings: 4

Cooking Time: 25 minutes

Ingredients:
- One tablespoon ground allspice
- One tablespoon ground cinnamon
- Half tablespoon ground ginger
- Half tablespoon onion powder
- Half tablespoon garlic powder
- A quarter tablespoon Cayenne pepper
- two ground cloves
- Three quarters tablespoon salt
- Half tablespoon ground black pepper freshly ground
- One pork tenderloin about 1 lb. trimmed of visible fat
- Two tablespoons white vinegar
- One tablespoon tomato paste

Directions: Mix the allspice, ginger, cinnamon, garlic powder, cayenne, onion powder, cloves, half a tsp of salt, and black pepper in a small bowl. Rub the mixture of spices over the pork and let it stand for 15 minutes.
Mix the tomato paste and the remaining quarter of a tablespoon of salt in another little cup.
Put the pork on the grill rack. At medium-high heat, grill, turning several times, until browned on all sides, for a total of 4 minutes.
Remove from the grill and put to a cooler section and continue to cook for 14 minutes.
Baste with vinegar and proceed to cook until a thermometer inserted into the thickest section reads 160 F.
Allow to cool for 5 minutes before slicing.

Nutrition: Calories: 169.3, Protein: 27.4g, Carbs: 5.7g, Fat: 5.9g, Sugar 3.7g

94.Pork Ribs

Preparation Time: 5 minutes
Servings: 4

Cooking Time: 30 minutes

Ingredients:
- Sixteen pork ribs
- Half cup hoisin sauce
- Two and a half tablespoon soy sauce
- One and a half tablespoon red wine vinegar

- *Two tablespoons Chinese spice powder*

Directions: Preheat the oven at 360 º F.
Cook the ribs in a large saucepan, coated with water. Carry the water to a boil and cook for twenty minutes.
Mix the soy sauce, hoisin sauce, wine vinegar, and spice powder in a small bowl.
Brush this glaze all over the ribs after draining the ribs.
Place and cook on a baking tray for 30 minutes.

Nutrition: Calories: 320.8, Protein: 22.2g, Carbs: 4.1g, Fat: 23.9g, Sugar: 2.2g

95.Pork Loin Roulades

Preparation Time: 10 minutes
Servings: 4

Cooking Time: 45 minutes

Ingredients:
- *2 lbs. of sliced pork loin*
- *2 garlic cloves*
- *8 sage leaves*
- *½ cup of dry white wine*
- *¼ cup of olive oil*
- *Salt and pepper to taste*

Directions: Flatten the pork slices, place a clove of garlic and a sage leaf on top, roll up and secure using a toothpick.
Heat the oil in a frying pan, place the roulades and brown over high heat on both sides, for even and homogeneous cooking. Lower the heat, add a little wine and water, salt and pepper to taste and leave to cook for about 30 minutes, until the meat is tender.

Nutrition: Calories: 164.8, Carbs: 1.1g, Protein: 22.8g, Fat: 9.1g

96.Roasted Pork and Apples

Preparation Time: 15 minutes
Servings: 4

Cooking Time: 35 minutes

Ingredients:
- *Salt and pepper to taste*
- *1/2 tsp. sage dried, crushed*
- *1 lb. pork tenderloin*
- *1 tbsp. canola oil*
- *1 onion, sliced into wedges*
- *3 cooking apples, sliced into wedges*
- *2/3 cup apple cider*
- *Sprigs fresh sage*

Directions: In a bowl, mix salt, pepper, and sage.
Season both sides of pork with this mixture.
Place a pan over medium heat. Brown both sides. Transfer to a roasting pan. Add the onion on top and around the pork.
Drizzle oil on top of the pork and apples. Roast in the oven at 425°F for 10 minutes.
Add the apples, roast for another 15 minutes.
In a pan, boil the apple cider and then simmer for 10 minutes.
Pour the apple cider sauce over the pork before serving.

Nutrition: Calories: 238.7, Fat: 5.8g, Protein: 24.7g, Carbs: 21.6g, Fiber: 3g, Sugar: 15.4g

97.Irish Pork Roast

Preparation Time: 40 minutes
Servings: 8

Cooking Time: 1 hour

Ingredients
- *1/2 lb. parsnips, peeled and sliced into small pieces*
- *1/2 lb. carrots, sliced into small pieces*
- *3 tbsp. olive oil, divided*
- *2 tsp. fresh thyme leaves, divided*
- *Salt and pepper to taste*
- *2 lb. pork loin roast*
- *1 cup dry hard cider Applesauce*

Directions: Preheat the oven to 400°F.
Drizzle half of the oil over the parsnips and carrots. Season with half of the thyme, salt, and pepper.
Arrange on a roasting pan. Rub the pork with the remaining oil.
Season with the remaining thyme, salt, and pepper. Put it on the roasting pan on top of the vegetables.

Roast for 60 minutes. Let cool before slicing.

Transfer the carrots and parsnips to a bowl and mix. Add the cider.

Place in a pan and simmer over low heat until the sauce has thickened.

Serve the pork with the vegetables and the applesauce.

Nutrition: Calories: 271.5, Fats: 7.7g, Protein: 24.2g, Carbs: 12.9g, Fibers: 6g, Sugar: 5.5g

98. Cranberry Pork Roast

Preparation Time: 20 minutes
Servings: 9

Cooking Time: 8 hours

Ingredients:
- 1/8 tsp. ground cloves
- 1/8 tsp. ground nutmeg
- 1 cup ground, or finely chopped, cranberries
- 1 tsp. orange peel, grated
- 2 3/4 lbs. boneless pork roast, trimmed of fat
- 3 tbsp. honey

Directions: Place the roast in a crockpot.

Mix the rest of the ingredients and pour over the roast.

Cover and cook on LOW for about 8 hours.

Nutrition: Calories: 213.8, Fat: 8.6g, Protein: 25.2g, Fibers: 1g, Carbs: 6.8g, Sugar: 6.5g

99. Crock Pork Tenderloin

Preparation Time: 5–15 minutes
Servings: 6

Cooking Time: 4 hours

Ingredients:
- 3/4 cup red wine
- 1 cup water
- 1 envelope salt-free onion soup mix
- 2 lbs. soft pork loin, cut in half lengthwise, visible fat removed
- 3 tbsp. light soy sauce
- 6 garlic cloves, peeled and chopped
- Freshly ground pepper to taste

Directions: Place the soft pork loin pieces in a crockpot. Pour wine, water, and soy sauce over the pork.

Turn the pork over in liquid several times to moisten.

Drizzle with dry onion soup mix. Top with chopped garlic and pepper.

Cover and cook on LOW for 4 hours.

Nutrition: Calories: 219.8, Fat: 3.8g, Protein: 37.5g, Fibers: 0g, Carbs: 5.6g, Sugar: 1.8g

100. Barbecue Pork Chops

Preparation Time: 5 minutes
Servings: 4

Cooking Time: 5 hours

Ingredients:
- 3 lbs. bone-in thick-cut pork chops
- 2–3 tbsp. barbecue seasoning
- 1/4 cup water

Directions: Cover each side of the pork chops with barbecue seasoning. Put them in the slow cooker.

Pour the water around the outside of the pork chops. Close the lid and cook on LOW for 5 hours.

Nutrition: Calories: 506.5, Fats: 19.7g, Protein: 72.3g, Fibers: 0g, Carbs: 3.7g, Sugar: 0g

101. Lime Pulled Pork

Preparation Time: 5 minutes
Servings: 4

Cooking Time: 35 minutes

Ingredients:
- 1 tbsp. chili adobo sauce
- 1 tbsp. chili powder
- 2 tsp. salt
- 1 tsp. garlic powder
- 1 tsp. cumin
- 1/2 tsp. pepper
- 1 lb. pork butt, cubed
- 1 tbsp. coconut oil
- 2 cups beef broth

- *1 lime, cut into wedges*
- *1/4 cup cilantro, chopped*

Directions: Mix the chili powder, pepper, garlic powder, cumin, salt, and sauce in a bowl.
Melt the oil on SAUTÉ in the instant pot. Rub the pork with the spice mixture.
Place the pork and sear for 3 minutes per side.
Add broth and close the lid. Press MANUAL and cook for 30 minutes.
Allow the natural release and open it. Shred the pork.
If you want crispy pork, then heat in a skillet. Serve warm with cilantro garnish and fresh lime wedges.

Nutrition: Calories: 569.3, Fats: 34.7g, Protein: 55.4g, Carbs: 1.9g

102. Mustard Pork Chops

Preparation Time: 5 minutes　　　　　　　　　　　　　　　　　**Cooking Time: 25 minutes**
Servings: 4

Ingredients:
- *¼ cup Dijon mustard*
- *1 tablespoon pure maple syrup*
- *2 tablespoons rice vinegar*
- *4 bone-in, thin-cut pork chops*

Directions: Preheat the oven to 400ºF.
In a small saucepan, combine the mustard, maple syrup, and rice vinegar. Stir to mix and bring to a simmer over medium heat. Cook for about 2 minutes until slightly thickened.
In a baking dish, place the pork chops and spoon the sauce over them, flipping to coat.
Bake, uncovered, for 18 to 22 minutes until the juices run clear.

Nutrition: Calories: 257.5, Fat: 6.9g, Protein: 39.5g, Carbs: 6.6g, Fiber: 0g, Sugar: 3.8g

103. Citrus Pork Tenderloin

Preparation Time: 10 minutes　　　　　　　　　　　　　　　　**Cooking Time: 30 minutes**
Servings: 4

Ingredients:
- *1/4 cup freshly squeezed orange juice*
- *2 teaspoons orange zest*
- *1 teaspoon low-sodium soy sauce*
- *1 teaspoon grated fresh ginger*
- *2 teaspoons minced garlic*
- *11/2 pounds (680 g) pork tenderloin roast, fat trimmed*
- *1 tablespoon extra-virgin olive oil*

Directions: Combine the orange juice and soy sauce, zest, ginger, and garlic in a large bowl. Stir to mix well.
Dunk the pork in the bowl and press to coat well.
Wrap the bowl in plastic and refrigerate to marinate for at least 2 hours.
Preheat the oven to 400°F. Detach the bowl from the refrigerator and discard the marinade.
Heat the olive oil in an oven-safe skillet over medium-high heat until shimmering.
Add the pork and sear for 5 minutes. Flip the pork halfway.
Arrange the skillet in the preheated oven and roast the pork for 25 minutes or until well browned.
Flip the pork halfway. Transfer the pork on a plate.
Let to cool before serving.

Nutrition: Calories: 227.5, Fat: 8.5g, Protein: 34.7g, Carbs: 3.1g, Fiber: 0g, Sugar: 0.7g

104. Pork Loin with Carrots

Preparation Time: 5 minutes　　　　　　　　　　　　　　　　　**Cooking Time: 40 minutes**
Servings: 4

Ingredients:
- *1 pound (454 g) pork loin*
- *1 tablespoon extra-virgin olive oil, divided*
- *¼ teaspoon freshly ground black pepper*
- *½ teaspoon dried rosemary*
- *4 (6-inch) carrots, chopped into ½-inch rounds*

Directions: Preheat the oven to 350ºF.
Rub the pork loin with ½ tablespoon of oil and season with the rosemary and pepper.
In a bowl, toss the carrots in the remaining ½ tablespoon of oil.

Place the pork and the carrots on a baking sheet in a single layer. Cook for 40 minutes.
Remove the baking sheet from the oven and let the pork rest for at least 10 minutes before slicing.
Divide the pork and carrots into four equal portions.

Nutrition: Calories: 343.5, Fat: 9.6g, Protein: 26.5g, Carbs: 15.1g, Fiber: 3.9g, Sugar: 4.1g

105. Pork and Apple Skillet

Preparation Time: 10 minutes
Servings: 4

Cooking Time: 20 minutes

Ingredients:
- 1 pound ground pork
- 1 red onion, thinly sliced
- 2 apples, peeled, cored, and thinly sliced
- 2 cups shredded cabbage
- 1 teaspoon dried thyme
- 2 garlic cloves, minced
- 1/4 cup apple cider vinegar
- 1 tablespoon Dijon mustard
- 1/2 teaspoon sea salt
- 1/8 teaspoon freshly ground black pepper

Directions: In a large skillet, cook the mince, crumbling it with a spoon, until browned.
Add the cabbage, onion, apples, and thyme to the fat in the pan. Cook the vegetables are soft, about 5 minutes.
Attach the garlic and cook, stirring constantly, for 5 minutes.
Set the pork to the pan.
In a small bowl, pour together the vinegar, mustard, salt, and pepper.
Add to the pan. Bring to a simmer. Cook, stirring, until the sauce begins to thicken, about 2 minutes.

Nutrition: Calories: 363.7, Fat: 23.2g, Carbs: 18.5g, Fiber: 3.6g, Protein: 20.3g

106. Pineapple Pork Tacos

Preparation Time: 15 minutes
Servings: 6

Cooking Time: 6 hours

Ingredients:
- 2 pounds Pork Loin Roast, fat trimmed
- 1/2 cup Lime Juice
- 1/3 cup Apple Juice
- 2 tsp. Paprika
- 2 tbsp. Vinegar
- 1 tbsp. Chili Powder
- 3/4 tsp. Salt
- 1/4 tsp. Black Pepper
- 2 cups diced Pineapple
- 1/4 cup diced Red Onion
- 2 cups Shredded Cabbage
- 1 cup diced Cucumber
- 12 Corn Tortillas

Directions: Combine the spices (set aside 1/4 tsp. salt) in a small bowl and rub all over the meat.
Set in the Slow Cooker and pour the apple juice around.
Put the lid on and cook on LOW for 6 hours.
In the meantime, combine the pineapple, remaining salt, cabbage, lime juice, cucumber, and onion. Place in a fridge until ready to serve. Open the lid and shred the pork.
Attach the vinegar to the meat and stir to coat well.
Serve the meat in tortillas, topped with the lime pineapple mixture.

Nutrition: Calories 305.7, Fats 4.7g, Carbs 30.5g, Protein 35.7g, Fiber: 4g

Fish and Seafood

107. Tuna with Olives

Preparation Time: 15 minutes
Servings: 4

Cooking Time: 14 minutes

Ingredients:
- 4 (6-ounce) (1-inch thick) tuna steaks
- 2 tablespoons extra-virgin olive oil, divided
- Salt and ground black pepper, as required
- 2 garlic cloves, minced
- 1 cup fresh tomatoes, chopped
- 1 cup dry white wine
- 2/3 cup green olives, pitted and sliced
- ¼ cup capers, drained
- 2 tablespoons fresh thyme, chopped
- 1½ tablespoons fresh lemon zest, grated
- 2 tablespoons fresh lemon juice
- 3 tablespoons fresh parsley, chopped

Directions: Preheat the grill to high heat. Grease the grill grate.
Coat the tuna steaks with 1 tablespoon of the oil and sprinkle with salt and black pepper.
Set aside for about 5 minutes.
For the sauce: in a small skillet, heat the remaining oil over medium heat and sauté the garlic for about 1 minute.
Add the tomatoes and cook for about 2 minutes. Stir in the wine and bring to a boil.
Add the remaining ingredients except parsley and cook, uncovered for about 5 minutes.
Stir in the parsley, salt and black pepper and remove from the heat.
Meanwhile, grill the tuna steaks over direct heat for about 1-2 minutes per side.
Serve the tuna steaks hot with the topping of sauce.

Nutrition: Calories: 467.5, Fat: 19.9g, Carbs: 7g, Sugar: 1.9g, Protein: 52.5g

108.   Stuffed Swordfish

Preparation Time: 15 minutes
Servings: 2

Cooking Time: 17 minutes

Ingredients:
- 1 (8-ounce) (2-inch thick) swordfish steak
- 1½ tablespoons olive oil, divided
- 1 tablespoon fresh lemon juice
- 2 cups fresh spinach, torn into bite size pieces
- 1 garlic clove, minced
- ¼ cup feta cheese, crumbled

Directions: Preheat the outdoor grill to high heat. Grease the grill grate.
Cut a slit on one side of fish steak to create a pocket.
In a bowl, add 1 tablespoon of the oil and lemon juice and mix.
Coat the both sides of fish with oil mixture evenly.
In a small skillet, add the remaining oil and garlic over medium heat and cook until heated.
Add the spinach and cook for about 2-3 minutes or until wilted.
Remove from the heat.
Stuff the fish pocket with spinach, followed by the feta cheese. Grill the fish pocket for about 8 minutes.
Flip and cook for about 5 minutes.
Cut the fish pocket into 2 equal sized pieces and serve.

Nutrition: Calories: 295.7, Fat: 16.5g, Carbs: 2.1g, Sugar: 0.7g, Protein: 32.9g

109.   Pesto Fish Fillet

Preparation Time: 10 minutes
Servings: 4

Cooking Time: 8 minutes

Ingredients:
- 4 halibut fillets
- 1/2 cup water
- 1 tbsp lemon zest, grated
- 1 tbsp capers
- 1/2 cup basil, chopped
- 1 tbsp garlic, chopped
- 1 avocado, peeled and chopped
- Pepper
- Salt

Directions: Add basil, lemon zest, capers, avocado, pepper, garlic, and salt into the blender and blend until smooth.
Place fish fillets on aluminum foil and spread a blended mixture on fish fillets.
Fold foil around the fish fillets.
Pour water into the instant pot and place trivet in the pot.
Place foil fish packet on the trivet. Seal pot with lid and cook on high for 8 minutes.
Once done, allow to release pressure. Remove lid.

Nutrition: Calories: 425.7, Fat: 16.1g, Carbs: 5.1g, Sugar: 0.3g, Protein: 62.7g

110.   Shrimp Zoodles

Preparation Time: 10 minutes
Servings: 4

Cooking Time: 5 minutes

Ingredients:
- 2 zucchini, spiralized
- 1 lb shrimp, peeled and deveined
- 1/2 tsp paprika
- 1 tbsp basil, chopped
- 1/2 lemon juice
- 1 tsp garlic, minced
- 2 tbsp olive oil
- 1 cup vegetable stock
- Pepper
- Salt

Directions: Add oil into the inner pot and set the instant pot on sauté mode. Add garlic and sauté for a minute.
Add shrimp and lemon juice and stir well and cook for 1 minute. Add remaining ingredients and stir well.
Seal pot with lid and cook on high for 3 minutes.
Once done, release pressure using quick release. Remove lid.

Nutrition: Calories: 214.7, Fat: 8.5g, Carbs: 5.2g, Sugar: 1.7g, Protein: 27.8g

111. Mediterranean Fish

Preparation Time: 15 minutes
Servings: 4

Cooking Time: 25 minutes

Ingredients:
- Two courgettes, trimmed, sliced into chunks
- Two Lebanese eggplants, trimmed, sliced into chunks
- 6 oz. capsicums, halved, seeded
- One thickly sliced red onion
- Two sliced garlic cloves
- Lemon juice
- One tablespoon olive oil
- 14 oz. of can diced tomatoes
- A quarter cup Kalamata olives
- A quarter cup parsley leaves
- A quarter cup dill, chopped
- Four pieces firm white fish fillets (6 oz. each one)
- One tablespoon of toasted pine nuts
- Couscous and lemon wedges for serving

Directions: Preheat the oven to 350°F. Using olive oil to spray a broad baking dish.
Combine the courgettes, capsicums, eggplants, garlic, ginger, and zest. Season.
Pour more than half of the juice and oil together and bake for 10 minutes.
Stir vegetables with tomatoes, olives, and half mixture of herbs. Add fish and drizzle with remaining oil.
Bake for 15 minutes. Serve with couscous and lemon wedges.

Nutrition: Calories: 420.7, Protein: 32.7g, Carbs: 29.8g, Fat: 17.5g, Sugar: 7.1g

112. Garlicky Shrimp

Preparation Time: 15 minutes
Servings: 4

Cooking Time: 6 minutes

Ingredients:
- 2 tablespoons olive oil
- 3 garlic cloves, sliced
- 1-pound shrimp, peeled and deveined
- 1 tablespoon fresh rosemary, chopped
- ½ teaspoon red pepper flakes, crushed
- Salt and ground black pepper, as required
- 1 tablespoon fresh lemon juice

Directions: In a large skillet, heat the oil over medium heat and sauté the garlic slices or about 2 minutes or until golden brown. Transfer the garlic slices into a bowl.
In the same skillet, add the shrimp, rosemary, red pepper flakes. salt and black pepper and cook for about 3-4 minutes, stirring frequently. Stir in the lemon juice and remove from the heat.
Serve hot with a topping of the garlic slices.

Nutrition: Calories: 201.7, Fat: 8.8g, Carbs: 2.8g, Sugar: 0.1g

113. Feta Tomato Sea Bass

Preparation Time: 10 minutes
Servings: 4

Cooking Time: 8 minutes

Ingredients:
- 4 sea bass fillets
- 1 1/2 cups water
- 1 tbsp olive oil
- 1 tsp garlic, minced
- 1 tsp basil, chopped
- 1 tsp parsley, chopped
- 1/2 cup feta cheese, crumbled
- 1 cup can tomatoes, diced
- Pepper
- Salt

Directions: Season fish fillets with pepper and salt.
Pour 2 cups of water into the instant pot then place steamer rack in the pot.
Place fish fillets on steamer rack in the pot. Seal pot with lid and cook on high for 5 minutes.
Once done, release pressure and remove the lid.
Remove fish fillets from the pot and clean the pot.
Add oil into the inner pot and set the instant pot on sauté mode. Add garlic and sauté for 1 minute.
Add parsley, tomatoes, and basil and stir well and cook for 1 minute.
Add fish fillets, top with crumbled cheese and cook for a minute.

Nutrition: Calories: 218.7, Fat: 9.7g, Carbs: 3.5g, Sugar: 2.1g, Protein: 26.7g

114. Codfish with Shrimp

Preparation Time: 10 minutes
Servings: 6

Cooking Time: 5 minutes

Ingredients:
- 1 lb codfish, cut into chunks
- 1 1/2 lbs shrimp
- 28 oz can tomatoes, diced
- 1 cup dry white wine
- 1 bay leaf
- 1 tsp cayenne
- 1 tsp oregano
- 1 shallot, chopped
- 1 tsp garlic, minced
- 1 tbsp olive oil
- 1/2 tsp salt

Directions: Add oil into the inner pot and set the instant pot on sauté mode. Add shallot and garlic and sauté for 2 minutes. Add wine, cayenne, bay leaf, oregano, and salt and cook for 3 minutes.
Add remaining ingredients and stir well.
Seal pot with a lid and select manual. Cook on low for 1 minute.
Once done, release pressure using quick release. Remove lid.

Nutrition: Calories: 280.7, Fat: 4.8g, Carbs: 9.8g, Sugar: 4.3g, Protein: 41.2g

115. Tartar Tuna Patties

Preparation Time: 5 minutes
Servings: 4

Cooking Time: 10 minutes

Ingredients:
- 1 pound (454 g) canned tuna, drained
- 1 cup whole-wheat bread crumbs
- 2 large eggs, lightly beaten
- Juice and zest of 1 lemon
- ½ onion, grated
- 1 tablespoon chopped fresh dill
- 3 tablespoons extra-virgin olive oil
- ½ cup tartar sauce, for topping

Directions: Mix together the tuna with the beaten eggs, onion, breadcrumbs, lemon juice and zest, and dill in a large bowl. Stir until well incorporated.
Scoop out the tuna mixture and shape into 4 equal-sized patties with your hands.
Transfer the patties to a plate and chill in the refrigerator for 10 minutes.
Once chilled, heat the olive oil in a large nonstick skillet over medium-high heat.
Add patties to the skillet and cook each side for 4 to 5 minutes.
Remove the patties from the heat and top with the tartar sauce.

Nutrition: Calories: 528.7g, Fat: 33.1g, Protein: 35.2g, Carbs: 17.7g, Fiber: 2.1g, Sugar: 3.3g

116. Fresh Rosemary Trout

Preparation Time: 5 minutes
Servings: 2

Cooking Time: 7 minutes

Ingredients:

- 4 to 6 fresh rosemary sprigs
- 8 ounces (227 g) trout fillets, about ¼ inch thick; rinsed and patted dry
- ½ teaspoon olive oil
- 1/8 teaspoon salt
- 1/8 teaspoon pepper
- 1 teaspoon fresh lemon juice

Directions: Preheat the oven to 350ºF. Put the rosemary sprigs in a small baking pan in a single row. Spread the fillets on the top of the rosemary sprigs. Brush both sides of each piece of fillet with the olive oil. Sprinkle with the salt, pepper, and lemon juice. Bake in the preheated oven for 7 minutes, or until the fish is opaque and flakes easily. Divide the fillets between two plates and serve hot.

Nutrition: Calories: 179.5g, Fat: 8.7g, Protein: 24.5g, Carbs: 0g, Fiber: 0g, Sugar: 0g

117. Blackened Shrimp

Preparation Time: 5 minutes
Servings: 4

Cooking Time: 5 minutes

Ingredients:
- 1 1/2 lbs. shrimp, peel & devein
- 4 lime wedges
- 4 tbsp. cilantro, chopped
- What you'll need from store cupboard:

- 4 cloves garlic, diced
- 1 tbsp. chili powder
- 1 tbsp. paprika
- 1 tbsp. olive oil
- 2 tsp. Splenda brown sugar
- 1 tsp. cumin
- 1 tsp. oregano
- 1 tsp. garlic powder
- 1 tsp. salt
- 1/2tsp. pepper

Directions: In a bowl combine seasonings and Splenda.
Heat oil in a skillet over med-high heat. Add shrimp and cook 1-2 minutes per side.
Add seasonings, and cook, stirring, 30 seconds. Serve garnished with a lime wedge and cilantro.

Nutrition: Calories: 251.7, Carbs: 6.8g, Protein: 39.7g, Fat: 6.8g, Sugar: 1.7g, Fiber: 1g

118. Cilantro Lime Grilled Shrimp

Preparation Time: 5 minutes
Servings: 6

Cooking Time: 5 minutes

Ingredients:
- 1 1/2 lbs. large shrimp raw, peeled, deveined with tails on
- Juice and zest of 1 lime
- 2 tbsp. fresh cilantro chopped
- What you'll need from store cupboard:
- ¼ cup olive oil
- 2 cloves garlic, diced fine
- 1 tsp. smoked paprika
- ¼ tsp. cumin
- 1/2 teaspoon salt
- ¼ tsp. cayenne pepper

Directions: Place the shrimp in a large Ziploc bag.
Mix remaining Ingredients in a small bowl and pour over shrimp. Let marinate 20-30 minutes.
Heat up the grill. Skewer the shrimp and cook 2 minutes, per side, just until they turn pick. Be careful not to overcook them. Serve garnished with cilantro.

Nutrition: Calories: 316.7, Carbs: 3.7g, Protein: 40.2g, Fat: 14.8g, Sugar: 0g, Fiber: 0g

119. Seared Sesame Tuna Steak

Preparation Time: 10 minutes
Servings: 2

Cooking Time: 20 minutes

Ingredients:
- Ahi tuna steaks – 2 (6-ounce)
- Soy sauce – 2 tablespoons
- Sesame oil – 1 tablespoon
- Sesame seeds – 1 teaspoon
- Salt – as per taste
- Pepper – as per taste

Directions: Begin by placing the tuna steak into a shallow dish, and season with pepper and salt.
Take a small bowl and add in the sesame oil and soy sauce. Whisk well and pour over the ahi tuna steak.
Flip over and set the dish aside for around 15 minutes at room temperature.
Take a nonstick pan and place it over a medium flame. Place the marinated ahi tuna steaks in the pan and cook for about 3 minutes per side. Once done, transfer onto a wooden block and slice into slices measuring about ½ inch in thickness. Transfer onto a serving platter and garnish with a sprinkle of black and white sesame seeds.

Nutrition: Fat: 8.7g, Protein: 40.9g, Carbs: 0.8g, Sugar: 0.2g

120. Alfredo Shrimp

Preparation Time: 10 minutes
Servings: 3

Cooking Time 10 minutes

Ingredients:
- Zucchini (spiral) – 4
- Olive oil – 1 tablespoon
- Shrimp (cleaned and peeled) – 1 pound
- Garlic (minced) – 2 cloves
- Butter (unsalted) – 2 tablespoons
- Heavy cream – ¾ cup
- Cream cheese – 4 ounces
- Fresh parmesan (grated) – ½ cup
- Salt – ¼ teaspoon
- Black pepper (ground) – ¼ teaspoon
- Fresh parsley – 2 tablespoons

Directions:
Start by placing a large nonstick skillet over a medium-high flame. Pour in the olive oil and let it heat through.
Once the oil is hot, toss in the shrimp and garlic. Cook for a couple of minutes.
Transfer onto a plate and set aside.
Return the pan to the heat and add in the butter and cream cheese. Whisk until both melt and are combined.

Add in the heavy cream, pepper, salt, and parmesan cheese; stir until well combined.
Now toss in the zucchini spiral noodles and cooked shrimp; cook with the cheese sauce for around 3 minutes.
Finish with a sprinkle of parmesan and serve.

Nutrition: Fat: 32.7g, Protein: 21.4g, Carbs: 6.8g, Sugar: 2.8g

121. Tilapia with Coconut Rice

Preparation Time: 5 minutes   **Cooking Time: 10 minutes**
Servings: 4

Ingredients:
- 4 (6-ounce) boneless tilapia fillets
- 1 tablespoon ground turmeric
- Salt and pepper
- 1 tablespoon olive oil
- 2 (8.8-ounce) packets precooked whole-grain rice
- 1 cup light coconut milk, shaken
- ½ cup fresh chopped cilantro
- 1 ½ tablespoons fresh lime juice

Directions: Season the fish with turmeric, salt, and pepper.
Heat the oil in a large skillet over medium heat and add the fish. Cook for 3 minutes per side until golden brown.
Remove the fillets to a plate and cover to keep warm.
Reheat the skillet and add the coconut milk, rice, and a pinch of salt.
Simmer on high heat until thickened, about 4 minutes.
Stir in the cilantro and lime juice. Spoon the rice onto plates and serve with cooked tilapia.

Nutrition: Calories: 459.2, Fat: 24.7g, Carbs: 26.7g, Protein: 35.2g, Sugar 2.1g, Fiber 3.7g

122. Grilled Tuna Kebabs

Preparation Time: 5 minutes   **Cooking Time: 10 minutes**
Servings: 4

Ingredients:
- 2 ½ tablespoons rice vinegar
- 2 tablespoons fresh grated ginger
- 2 tablespoons sesame oil
- 2 tablespoons soy sauce
- 2 tablespoons fresh chopped cilantro
- 1 tablespoon minced green chili
- 1 ½ pounds fresh tuna, cut into 1 ¼-inch cubes
- 1 red pepper, cut into 1-inch pieces
- 1 red onion, cut into 1-inch pieces

Directions: Whisk together the rice vinegar, sesame oil, soy sauce, ginger, cilantro, and chili in a medium bowl – add a few drops of liquid stevia extract to sweeten.
Toss in the tuna and chill for 20 minutes, covered.
Meanwhile, grease a grill pan with cooking spray and soak wooden skewers in water.
Slide the tuna cubes onto the skewers with red pepper and onion.
Grill for 3 minutes on each side until done to your liking and serve hot.

Nutrition: Calories: 239.7, Fat: 8.7g, Carbs: 8.1g, Protein: 32.1g, Sugar 3.1g, Fiber 1.7g

123. Chili Lime Cod

Preparation Time: 10 minutes   **Cooking Time: 10 minutes**
Servings: 2

Ingredients:
- 1/3 c. coconut flour
- 1/2 tsp. cayenne pepper
- 1 egg, beaten
- 1 lime
- 1 tsp. crushed red pepper flakes
- 1 tsp. garlic powder
- 12 oz. cod fillets
- Sea salt & pepper, to taste

Directions: Preheat the oven to 400° F and line a baking sheet with non-stick foil.
Place the flour in a plate and drag the fillets through the beaten egg.
Dredge the cod in the coconut flour, then lay on the baking sheet.
Sprinkle the tops of the fillets with the seasoning and lime juice.
Bake for 10 minutes until the fillets are flaky.

Nutrition: Calories: 214.5, Fat: 4.6g, Carbs: 2.8g, Protein: 37.5g

124. Sesame-Crusted Tuna with Green Beans

Preparation Time: 15 minutes
Servings: 4

Cooking Time: 10 minutes

Ingredients:
- 1/4 cup white sesame seeds
- 1/4 cup black sesame seeds
- 4 (6-ounce) ahi tuna steaks
- Salt and pepper
- 1 tablespoon olive oil
- 1 tablespoon coconut oil
- 2 cups green beans

Directions: In a shallow dish, mix the two kinds of sesame seeds.

Season the tuna with pepper and salt. Dredge the tuna in a mixture of sesame seeds.

Heat up to high heat the olive oil in a skillet, then add the tuna.

Cook for 2 minutes, then sear on the other side.

Remove the tuna from the skillet, and let it rest while using the coconut oil to heat the skillet.

Fry the green beans in the oil for 5 minutes then use sliced tuna to eat.

Nutrition: Calories: 379.4, Fat: 18.5g, Protein: 44.9g, Carbs: 7.9g, Fiber 3g

Soups

125. Carrot Ginger Soup

Preparation Time: 5 minutes
Servings: 4

Cooking Time: 20 minutes

Ingredients:

- *1 tablespoon olive oil*
- *1 medium yellow onion, chopped*
- *3 cups fat-free chicken broth*
- *1 pound carrots, peeled and chopped*
- *1 tablespoon fresh grated ginger*
- *¼ cup fat-free sour cream*
- *Salt and pepper*

Directions: Heat the oil in a large saucepan over medium heat.
Add the onions and sauté for 5 minutes until softened.
Stir in the broth, carrots, and ginger then cover and bring to a boil
Reduce heat and simmer for 20 minutes. Stir in the sour cream then remove from heat.
Blend using an immersion blender until smooth and creamy. Season with salt and pepper then serve hot.

Nutrition: Calories: 269.6, Fat: 22.1g, Carbs: 10.9g

126. Mushroom Soup

Preparation Time: 10 minutes
Servings: 2

Cooking Time: 20 minutes

Ingredients:

- 1 cup Cremini mushrooms, chopped
- 1 cup Cheddar cheese, shredded
- 2 cups of water
- ½ teaspoon salt
- 1 teaspoon dried thyme
- ½ teaspoon dried oregano
- 1 tablespoon fresh parsley, chopped
- 1 tablespoon olive oil
- 1 bell pepper, chopped

Directions: Pour olive oil in the pan. Add mushrooms and bell pepper. Roast the vegetables for 5 minutes over the medium heat. Then sprinkle them with thyme, salt, and dried oregano. Add parsley and water. Stir the soup well. Cook the soup for 10 minutes.
After this, blend the soup until it is smooth and simmer it for 5 minutes more. Add cheese and stir.

Nutrition: Calories: 319.7, Fat: 25.7g, Carbs: 7g, Protein: 16.2g

127. Vegetable Beef Soup

Preparation Time: 10 minutes
Servings: 4

Cooking Time: 15 minutes

Ingredients:

- 1 pound ground beef
- 1 onion, chopped
- 2 celery stalks, chopped
- 1 carrot, chopped
- 1 teaspoon dried rosemary
- 6 cups low-sodium beef or chicken broth
- 1/2 teaspoon sea salt
- 1/8 teaspoon freshly ground black pepper
- 2 cups peas

Directions: Cook the ground beef, crumbling with the side of a spoon, until browned, about 5 minutes.
Add the onion, celery, carrot, and rosemary. Cook, stirring, until the vegetables start to soften, about 5 minutes.
Add the broth, salt, pepper, and peas. Bring to a simmer. Reduce the heat and simmer, stirring, until warmed through, about 5 minutes more.

Nutrition: Calories: 354.7, Fat: 16.5g, Carbs: 17.5, Fiber: 5g, Protein: 34.5g

128. 7-Minutes Egg Drop Soup

Preparation Time: 5 minutes
Servings: 4

Cooking Time: 7 minutes

Ingredients:

- Chicken broth – 4 cups
- Coconut aminos – 4 teaspoons
- Mushrooms (thinly sliced) – 8 medium
- Green onions (thinly sliced) – 4 medium
- Fresh ginger (grated) – 1 teaspoon
- Black pepper – 1 teaspoon
- Eggs – 4 large
- Sea salt – as per taste

Directions: Start by adding the chicken broth, coconut aminos, ginger, mushrooms, black pepper, and onions into a medium-sized saucepan.
Place the pan on a high flame and let it come to a boil. Reduce the flame and cook for a couple of minutes more. Crack the eggs in a cup and whisk them well.
Slowly pour the whisked eggs in a stream into the simmering soup. Keep stirring to get some smooth egg ribbons. Stir in the salt as soon as you finish cooking the soup.

Nutrition: Calories: 107, Fat: 5.8g, Protein: 10.7g, Carbs: 4.8g, Sugar: 0.9g

129. Classic Tomato Soup

Preparation Time: 10 minutes
Servings: 4

Cooking Time: 15 minutes

Ingredients:

- Water – 1 ½ cups
- Brown sugar – 2 tsp
- Vegetable oil – 2 tsp
- Chopped onion – ¼ cup
- Chopped celery – ¼ cup
- Diced tomatoes – 15oz / 425g
- Salt - ½ tsp
- Dried basil – ½ tsp
- Ground pepper – ¼ tsp
- Dried oregano – ¼ tsp

Directions: Take a large skillet and heat some oil. Put onion and celery then cook for 4 minutes. Include the other ingredients. Boil and simmer for 10 minutes.
Garnish with basil and serve.

Nutrition: Calories: 75.4, Fat: 1.8g, Fiber: 4g, Sugar: 5.8g, Carbs: 12.7g, Protein 2.3g

130. Creamy Tomato Soup

Preparation Time: 10 minutes
Servings: 4

Cooking Time: 50 minutes

Ingredients:
- Fresh tomatoes – 1 pound
- Garlic (peeled) – 4 cloves
- Olive oil – ¼ cup
- Chicken broth – 4 cups
- Heavy cream – ½ cup
- Salt – as per taste
- Pepper – as per taste

Directions: Start by preheating the oven by setting the temperature to 400° F.
Take a baking sheet and line it with an aluminum foil sheet.
Remove the core of the tomatoes and place them on the lined baking sheet. Place the garlic cloves alongside the tomatoes.
Season both tomatoes and garlic with pepper and salt, and drizzle with olive oil.
Place the baking sheet into the preheated oven and roast for around 30 minutes.
Transfer the roasted tomatoes and garlic along with the juices and 2 cups of broth into the blender.
Blend the tomatoes and garlic into a smooth puree-like consistency.
Take a large saucepan and place it over a medium flame. Pour the prepared tomato puree into the saucepan.
Stir in the heavy cream and remaining broth; cook over a medium flame for around 10 minutes.
Season with black pepper and salt as per your taste. Mix well.
Transfer into a bowl and garnish with a dash of cream and freshly cracked pepper.

Nutrition: Calories: 123, Fat: 19.1g, Protein: 6.9g, Carbs: 6.1g, Sugar: 3.2g

131. Fresh Broccoli Soup

Preparation Time: 20 minutes
Servings: 8

Cooking Time: 45 minutes

Ingredients:
- Broccoli – 1 ½ lb. / 680g
- Vegetable oil - 1 tbsp.
- Chopped onion – ¼ cup
- 1 Minced garlic – 1 clove
- Vegetable broth – 32oz / 907g
- Water – 2 cups
- Lime juice – 2 tbsp.
- Sliced mushrooms – ½ lb. / 227g
- Soy sauce – 1tbsp
- 2 Chopped carrots
- 2 Chopped celery ribs

Directions: Cut the broccoli in to small pieces.
Then take a frying pan and add oil. Fry the mushrooms for 5 minutes.
Stir with soy sauce and take off from the heat.
Put broccoli, carrots, onion, water, celery, garlic and broth to the same pan.
Let it boil and simmer for 30 minutes. Blend the hard remaining vegetables in the soup.
Put it back to the pot and add cauliflower and mushrooms.
Cook for another 8 minutes and turn off the heat.

Nutrition: Calories: 68.7, Fat: 1.7g, Fiber: 3g, Sugar: 3.8g, Carbs: 10.8g, Protein 4.1g

132. Low Carb Cream Bouillon

Preparation Time: 5 minutes
Servings: 4

Cooking Time: 25 minutes

Ingredients:
- Chicken breast – 1lb / 454g
- Taco seasoning – 1 tbsp.
- Cream cheese – 8oz / 227g
- Heavy cream – ½ cup
- Salt to taste
- Chicken broth – 3 cups
- Avocado oil – 1 tbsp.
- Diced chilies – 10oz / 283g

Directions: Take a pot and heat the oil.

Put taco seasoning and diced chilies, and cook for a minute.

Include the broth and chicken. Simmer for 20 minutes.

Keep the chicken pot away. Add cream cheese and heavy cream to the bouillon. Add the salt to taste and serve.

Nutrition: Calories: 478.5, Fat: 36.8g, Fiber: 1g, Sugar: 3.8g, Carbs 6.8g, Protein 30.2g

133.   Mashed Peas Goulash

Preparation Time: 10 minutes   **Cooking Time: 1 hour**
Servings: 8

Ingredients:
- Dried green peas – 1lb / 454g
- 1 Chopped carrot
- Salt – 1 ½ tsp
- Thyme – ½ tsp
- Pepper – ½ tsp
- Water – 6 cups
- 1 Chopped celery
- 1 Chopped onion
- 1 Bay leaf

Directions: Take a cooking pot and put all the ingredients.

Cook for one hour at medium heat until the peas become softer.

Remove the bay leaves and serve.

Nutrition: Calories: 201.8, Fat: 0.9g, Fiber: 15g, Sugar: 4.7g, Carbs: 35.4g, Protein 14.3g

Lunch and Dinner

134. Pork Chops with Apples and Red Cabbage

Preparation Time: 15 minutes
Serving: 4

Cooking Time: 30 minutes

Ingredients:

- ¼ cup apple cider vinegar
- 2 tablespoons granulated sweetener
- 4 (4-ounce) pork chops, about 1 inch thick
- 1 tablespoon extra-virgin olive oil
- ½ red cabbage, finely shredded
- 1 sweet onion, thinly sliced
- 1 apple, peeled, cored, and sliced
- 1 teaspoon chopped fresh thyme

Direction: Scourge together the vinegar and sweetener. Set it aside.
Season the pork with salt and pepper.
Position huge skillet over medium-high heat and add the olive oil.
Cook the pork chops until no longer pink, turning once, about 8 minutes per side.
Put chops aside.
Add the cabbage and onion to the skillet and sauté until the vegetables have softened, about 5 minutes.
Add the vinegar mixture and the apple slices to the skillet and bring the mixture to a boil.
Reduce heat to low and simmer, covered, for 5 additional minutes.
Return the pork chops to the skillet, along with any accumulated juices and thyme, cover, and cook for 5 minutes.

Nutrition: Calories: 222.7, Carbs: 11.3g, Fiber: 3g

135. Coconut Flour Tortillas

Preparation Time: 10 minutes
Servings: 4

Cooking Time: 15 minutes

Ingredients:

- 3/4 cup egg whites
- 1/3 cup water
- 1/4 cup coconut flour
- 1 tsp. sunflower oil
- 1/2 tsp. salt
- 1/2 tsp. cumin
- 1/2 tsp. chili powder

Directions: Add all the ingredients, except oil, to a food processor and pulse until combined. Let rest for 7–8 minutes.
Heat the oil in a large skillet over med-low heat. Pour 1/4 cup batter into the center and tilt to spread to 7–8-inch circle.
When the top is no longer shiny, flip the tortilla and cook for 1–2 minutes. Repeat with the remaining batter.
Place each tortilla on parchment paper and lightly wipe off excess oil.

Nutrition: Calories: 26.5, Carbs: 0.9g, Protein: 5.3g, Fat: 0g, Sugar: 0g, Fiber: 0g

136. Beer Bread

Preparation Time: 5 minutes
Servings: 14

Cooking Time: 45 minutes

Ingredients:

- 1/4 cup butter, soft
- 12 oz. light beer
- 3 cup low-carb baking mix
- 1/3 cup Splenda

Directions: Heat oven to 375ºF. Use 1 tbsp. of butter to grease the bottom of a 9x5-inch loaf pan.
In a large bowl, whisk together baking mix, beer, and Splenda. Pour into the prepared pan.
Bake for 45 minutes. Cool in pan 10 minutes, remove from pan, and cool on wire rack.
Melt the remaining butter in a microwave and brush over a warm loaf in a small glass bowl; cool for 15 minutes before slicing.

Nutrition: Calories: 161.7, Carbs: 15.9g, Protein: 9.3g, Fat: 4.9g, Sugar: 4.6g, Fiber: 4g

137. Chickpea Soup

Preparation Time: 15 minutes
Servings: 2

Cooking Time: 35 minutes

Ingredients:
- 1 lb. cooked chickpeas
- 1 lb. vegetables, chopped
- 1 cup low-sodium vegetable broth
- 2 tbsp. mixed herbs

Directions: mix all the ingredients in an instant pot.
Cook on STEW for 35 minutes.
Release the pressure naturally.

Nutrition: Calories: 309.8, Carbs: 19.8g, Sugar: 2.8g, Fat: 4.7g, Protein: 27.3g

138. Butter Sautéed Green Beans

Preparation Time: 15 minutes
Servings: 4

Cooking Time: 5 minutes

Ingredients:
- 1 tbsp. butter
- 1 1/2 lbs. green beans, trimmed
- 1 tsp. ground nutmeg
- Sea salt, to taste

Directions: Melt the butter in a large skillet over medium heat.
Sauté the green beans in the melted butter for 5 minutes until tender but still crisp, stirring.
Season with nutmeg and salt and mix well. Remove from the heat and cool for a few minutes before serving.

Nutrition: Calories: 82.6, Fat: 3g, Protein: 3.7g, Carbs: 11.8g, Fiber: 6.1g, Sugar: 2.8g

139. Tender Veggie Spring Peas

Preparation Time: 10 minutes
Servings: 6 (1/2 cup each)

Cooking Time: 11 minutes

Ingredients:
- 1 tbsp. unsalted butter
- 1/2 Vidalia onion, thinly sliced
- 1 cup low-sodium vegetable broth
- 3 cups fresh shelled peas
- 1 tbsp. fresh tarragon, minced

Directions: Melt the butter in a skillet over medium heat.
Sauté the onion in the melted butter for 3 minutes, stir occasionally.
Pour in the vegetable broth and whisk well. Add the peas and tarragon to the skillet and stir to combine.
Reduce the heat to low, cover, and cook for 8 minutes more.
Let the peas cool for 5 minutes and serve warm.

Nutrition: Calories: 81.5, Fat: 1.8g, Protein: 4.7g, Carbs: 11.7g, Fiber: 3.8g, Sugar: 4.1g

140. Eggplant and Bulgur Pilaf

Preparation Time: 10 minutes
Servings: 4

Cooking Time: 60 minutes

Ingredients:
- 1 tbsp. extra-virgin olive oil
- 1/2 sweet onion, chopped
- 2 tsp. garlic, minced
- 1 cup eggplant, chopped
- 1 1/2 cups bulgur
- 4 cups low-sodium chicken broth
- 1 cup tomato, diced
- Sea salt and freshly ground black pepper, to taste
- 2 tbsp. fresh basil, chopped

Directions: Place a large saucepan over medium-high heat. Add the oil and sauté the onion and garlic until softened and translucent, about 3 minutes.
Stir in the eggplant and sauté 4 minutes to soften.
Stir in the broth, bulgur, and tomatoes. Bring the mixture to a boil.
Reduce the heat to low, cover, and simmer until the water has been absorbed, about 50 minutes.
Season the pilaf with salt and pepper. Garnish with the basil and serve.

Nutrition: Calories: 299.8, Fat: 3.8g, Protein: 14.7g, Carbs: 53.7g, Fiber: 12g, Sugar: 6.7g

141. Filled Chicken Breast

Preparation Time: 5 minutes
Servings: 1

Cooking Time: 20 minutes

Ingredients:
* 1 Chicken breast – ½ lb. / 227g
* Mozzarella cheese
* Paprika – ¼ teaspoon
* Pepper – 1 pinch
* Toothpicks
* Chopped tomato– 1 teaspoon
* 5 Basil leaves
* Garlic – 1 clove
* Curry powder – ¼ teaspoon

Directions: Take the chicken breast and cut in half to form a pocket.
In a bowl mix tomato, mozzarella, basil and garlic.
Fill the mixture in to the chicken pocket you make.
You can use toothpicks to seal the pocket.
Put the chicken breast filled with the filling in a baking sheet and sprinkle pepper, paprika and curry powder.
Set the oven temperature at 365F 185C and bake it for 20 minutes.
You should remove toothpicks prior to serving.

Nutrition: Calories: 262.7, Fat: 3.7g, Fiber: 2.4g, Sugar: 0.9g, Carbs: 7.9g, Protein: 46.2g

142. Onion and Zucchini Platter

Preparation Time: 15 minutes
Servings: 4

Cooking Time: 45 minutes

Ingredients:
* 3 large zucchinis, julienned
* 1 cup cherry tomatoes, halved
* 1/2 cup basil
* 2 red onions, thinly sliced
* 1/4 tsp. salt
* 1 tsp. cayenne pepper
* 2 tbsp. lemon juice

Directions: Make zucchini noodles using a vegetable peeler and shave the zucchini with a peeler lengthwise until you get to the core and seeds.
Turn zucchini and repeat until you have long strips. Discard seeds.
Lay strips on a chopping board and slice lengthwise to your required thickness.
Mix noodles in a bowl alongside onion, basil, tomatoes, and toss.
Sprinkle cayenne pepper and salt on top and drizzle the juice.

Nutrition: Calories: 155.7, Fat: 7.6g, Carbs: 5.6g, Protein: 7.3g

143. Ginger Soup

Preparation Time: 10 minutes
Servings: 4

Cooking Time: 10 minutes

Ingredients:
* 1 can tomatoes, diced
* 1 can peppers
* 6 cups vegetable broth
* 3 cups green onions, diced
* 2 cups mushrooms, sliced
* 3 tsp. garlic, minced
* 3 tsp. ginger, fresh and grated
* 4 tbsp. tamari
* 2 cups bok choy, chopped
* 1 tbsp. cilantro, chopped
* 3 tbsp. carrot, grated

Directions: Add all the ingredients apart from carrots and scallions into a saucepan, then bring it to a boil using medium-high heat.
Lower to medium-low, cooking for 6 minutes.
Stir in your carrots and green onions, cooking for an additional 2 minutes. Serve with cilantro.

Nutrition: Calories: 381.7, Fat: 35.4g, Carbs: 8.8g, Protein: 7.3g

144. Creamy Chicken

Preparation Time: 12 minutes
Servings: 2

Cooking Time: 13 minutes

Ingredients:
* 1/2 small onion, chopped
* 1/4 cup sour cream
* 1 tbsp. butter
* 1/4 cup mushrooms
* 1/2 lb. chicken breasts

Directions: Heat butter in a skillet and add onions and mushrooms.
Sauté for 5 minutes and add chicken breasts and salt.
Close the lid and cook for 5 more minutes. Add the soured cream and cook for 3 minutes.
Open the lid and serve in a dish to eat immediately.
Transfer the creamy chicken breasts into a dish and put them aside to chill for meal prepping.
Divide it into 2 containers and cover them. Refrigerate for 2–3 days and reheat in microwave before serving.

Nutrition: Calories: 334.7, Carbs: 2.3g, Protein: 34.5g, Fat: 19.5g, Sugar: 0.7g

145. Chicken Tortilla Soup

Preparation Time: 10 minutes　　　　　　　　　　　　　　　　**Cooking Time: 20 minutes**
Servings: 6

Ingredients:
- 1 tablespoon olive oil
- ½ small yellow onion, diced
- 3 cloves minced garlic
- 2 cups fat-free chicken broth
- 1 (15-ounce) can black beans, rinsed and drained
- 1 cup crushed tomatoes
- 2 tablespoons tomato paste
- 1 teaspoon ground cumin
- ½ teaspoon paprika
- Salt and pepper
- 8 ounces cooked chicken breast, shredded
- 1 tablespoon fresh lime juice
- 1 tablespoon fresh chopped cilantro
- 1 medium diced avocado, optional

Directions: Heat the oil in a large saucepan over medium heat.
Add the onion and sauté for 3 minutes then stir in the garlic and cook 1 minute more.
Pour in the chicken broth, beans, tomatoes, tomato paste, cumin, and paprika.
Bring to a light boil then simmer for 10 minutes.
Sprinkle with salt and pepper and stir in the cooked chicken.
Cook until the chicken is heated through then remove from heat.
Stir in the cilantro and lime juice then adjust seasoning to taste. Serve hot with diced avocado.

Nutrition: Calories: 409.6, Fat: 10.4g, Carbs: 52.6g, Protein: 27.9g, Sugar: 4.6g, Fiber 14.8g

146. Beef Salad

Preparation Time: 20 minutes　　　　　　　　　　　　　　　　**Cooking Time: 8 minutes**
Servings: 6

Ingredients:
For Steak:
- 1½ pounds skirt steak, trimmed and cut into 4 pieces
- Salt and ground black pepper, as required

For Salad:
- 2 medium green bell pepper, seeded and sliced thinly
- 2 large tomatoes, sliced
- 1 cup onion, sliced thinly
- 8 cups mixed fresh baby greens

For Dressing:
- 2 teaspoons Dijon mustard
- 4 tablespoons balsamic vinegar
- ½ cup olive oil
- Salt and ground black pepper, as required

Directions: Preheat the grill to medium-high heat. Grease the grill grate.
Sprinkle the beef steak with a little salt and black pepper.
Place the steak onto the grill and cook, covered for about 3-4 minutes per side.
Transfer the steak onto a cutting board for about 10 minutes before slicing.
Meanwhile, in a large bowl, mix together all salad ingredients.
For dressing: in another bowl, add all the ingredients and beat until well combined.
Pour the dressing over salad and toss to coat well.
Divide the salad onto serving plates evenly.
Top each plate with the steak slices and serve.

Nutrition: Calories: 312.7, Fat: 20.9g, Carbs: 6.2g, Sugar: 3.1g, Fiber: 1.7g, Protein: 24.5g

Sauces and Dressing

147. Alfredo Sauce

Preparation Time: 10 minutes
Servings: 6

Cooking Time: 10 minutes

Ingredients:
- 1/4 cup butter, grass-fed
- 1 cup cream cheese
- 1 1/2 cups heavy (whipping) cream
- 2 tsp. garlic, minced
- 1/4 tsp. salt
- 1/4 tsp. freshly ground black pepper
- 1 cup Parmesan cheese, grated

Directions: In a medium saucepan over medium heat, stir together the butter, cream cheese, and cream. Cook, stirring until the sauce is smooth and the butter and cheese are melted.
Add the garlic, salt, and pepper and whisk until well blended. Whisk in the Parmesan. Bring sauce to a boil and cook until slightly thickened about 5 minutes.
Cool the sauce completely and store it in a sealed container in the refrigerator for up to 3 days.

Nutrition: Calories: 477.5, Fat: 47.6g, Protein: 10.2g, Carbs: 38g, Fiber: 0g

148. Sriracha Peanut Sauce

Preparation Time: 5 minutes

Servings: 4

Ingredients:
- 1/2 cup creamy peanut butter
- 2 tbsp. soy sauce (or coconut aminos)
- 1 tsp. Sriracha sauce
- 1 tsp. toasted sesame oil
- 1 tsp. garlic powder

Directions: In a blender, blend the Sriracha sauce, peanut butter, sesame oil, soy sauce, and garlic powder until thoroughly mixed.
Pour into an airtight glass container and keep in the refrigerator for up to 1 week.

Nutrition: Calories: 184.7, Fat: 14.7g, Protein: 7.3g, Carbs: 7.5g, Fiber: 2g

149. Salsa de Queso

Preparation Time: 10 minutes
Servings: 4

Cooking Time: 3 hours

Ingredients:
- 1 tbsp. extra-virgin olive oil
- 12 oz. (340 g.) cream cheese
- 1 cup sour cream
- 2 cups salsa verde
- 1 cup Monterey Jack cheese, shredded

Directions: Lightly grease the container of the slow cooker with olive oil.
Stir together the salsa verde, sour cream, cream cheese, and Monterey Jack cheese in a large bowl until blended.
Transfer the mixture to the container.
Cover and cook on LOW for 3 hours. Serve warm.

Nutrition: Calories: 277.6, Fat: 24.5g, Protein: 9.3g, Carbs: 3.7g, Fiber: 0g

150. Aioli

Preparation Time: 10 minutes

Servings: 8

Ingredients:
- 1 large egg
- 2 tsp. Dijon mustard
- 1 1/2 tsp. garlic, minced
- 1 cup olive oil
- 1 tbsp. lemon juice, freshly squeezed
- Sea salt to taste, for seasoning

Directions: In a medium bowl, whisk together the egg, mustard, and garlic until they're well blended, about 2 minutes.
Add the olive oil, constantly whisking until the aioli is thick. Whisk in the lemon juice and season with salt.
Store the aioli in an airtight container in the refrigerator for up to 4 days.

Nutrition: Calories: 123.7, Fat: 13.8g, Protein: 0g, Carbs: 0g, Fiber: 0g

151. Sriracha Mayonnaise

Preparation Time: 5 minutes

Servings: 4

Ingredients:
- 1/2 cup mayonnaise
- 2 tbsp. Sriracha sauce
- 1/2 tsp. garlic powder
- 1/2 tsp. onion powder
- 1/4 tsp. paprika

Directions: In a small bowl, whisk all the ingredients until well mixed.
Pour into an airtight glass container, and keep in the refrigerator for up to 1 week.

Nutrition: Calories: 200.5, Fat: 21.7g, Protein: 1.3g, Carbs: 1.9g, Fiber: 1g

152. Ketchup

Preparation Time: 10 minutes
Servings: 2 cups

Cooking Time: 6–7 hours

Ingredients:
- 1 tbsp. extra-virgin olive oil
- 1 can (28 oz./794 g.) crushed tomatoes
- 1/2 cup apple cider vinegar
- 1/4 cup granulated erythritol
- 1 sweet onion, finely chopped
- 2 tsp. garlic, minced
- 1/4 tsp. allspice
- 1/8 tsp. ground cloves
- 1/8 tsp. celery salt
- 2 bay leaves

Directions: Lightly grease the container of the slow cooker with olive oil.
Add the rest of the ingredients to the container.
Cook uncovered for 6–7 hours on low, until thick.
Remove the bay leaves. Use a regular blender to purée the mixture.
Cool and transfer the ketchup to jars, seal, and refrigerate.
Store the ketchup in the refrigerator for up to 1 week or in the freezer for 2 months.

Nutrition: Calories: 16.8, Fat: 0.8g, Protein: 0g, Carbs: 1.8, Fiber: 1g

153. Ranch Dressing

Preparation Time: 10 minutes   **Servings: 8–10**

Ingredients:
- 8 oz. (227 g.) fat-free plain Greek yogurt
- 1/4 cup low-fat buttermilk
- 1 tbsp. garlic powder
- 1 tbsp. dill, dried
- 1 tbsp. chives, dried
- 1 tbsp. onion powder
- 1 tbsp. parsley, dried
- Pinch freshly ground black pepper

Directions: In a shallow, medium bowl, combine the Greek yogurt and buttermilk.
Stir in the garlic powder, dill, chives, onion powder, parsley, and pepper and mix well.
Serve with animal protein or vegetable of your choice, or place in an airtight container.

Nutrition: Calories: 29.8, Fat: 0g, Protein: 3.5g, Carbs: 2.8g, Fiber: 0g, Sugar: 1.9g

---

154. Italian Vinaigrette

Preparation Time: 5 minutes   **Servings: 4**

Ingredients:
- 1/4 cup extra-virgin olive oil
- 2 tbsp. red wine vinegar
- 1 tsp. Dijon mustard
- 2 tsp. Italian seasoning
- 1 garlic clove, finely minced
- 1 tbsp. shallot, minced
- 1/4 tsp. sea salt
- 1/8 tsp. freshly ground black pepper

Directions: Stir together all ingredients in a medium bowl until completely mixed and emulsified.

Nutrition: Calories: 128.7, Fat: 13.9g, Protein: 0g, Carbs: 0.8g, Fiber: 0.8g, Sugar: 0.1g

---

155. Lemony Dill and Yogurt Dressing

Preparation Time: 5 minutes   **Servings: 2/3 cup**

Ingredients:
- 2 tbsp. mayonnaise
- 1 tsp. freshly squeezed lemon juice
- 1 tsp. fresh dill, chopped
- 1/2 cup plain Greek yogurt
- 1/4 tsp. garlic powder
- 1/4 tsp. salt

Directions: Combine all the ingredients in a bowl. Stir to mix well.

Nutrition: Calories: 35.7, Fat: 0.9g, Protein: 3.5g, Carbs: 2.8g, Fiber: 0g, Sugar: 1.6g

---

156. Avocado Cilantro Dressing

Preparation Time: 5 minutes   **Servings: 1 cup**

Ingredients:
- 1 large avocado, peeled and pitted
- 1/2 cup plain Greek yogurt
- 3/4 cup fresh cilantro
- 1 tbsp. water
- 2 tsp. lime juice, freshly squeezed
- 1/8 tsp. garlic powder
- Pinch salt

Directions: Process the avocado, yogurt, cilantro, water, lime juice, garlic powder, and salt in a blender until creamy and emulsified.
Chill for 30 minutes in the refrigerator to let the flavors blend.

Nutrition: Calories: 91.8, Fat: 6.2g, Protein: 4.5g, Carbs: 4.2g, Fiber: 2.3g, Sugar: 0.7g

---

157. Spicy Dipping Sauce

Preparation Time: 5 minutes   **Servings: 1/2 cup**

Ingredients:
- 1/3 cup low-fat mayonnaise
- 1–2 tsp. hot sauce, to your liking
- 2 tsp. rice vinegar
- 1 tsp. sesame oil

Directions: Stir together the mayo, hot sauce, rice vinegar, and oil in a small bowl until thoroughly smooth.

Chill for at least 30 minutes to blend the flavors.

Nutrition: Calories: 53.7, Fat: 4.3g, Protein: 0g, Carbs: 1.5g, Fiber: 0g, Sugar: 0.7g

158. Maple Shallot Vinaigrette

Preparation Time: 3 minutes   **Cooking Time: 5 minutes**
Servings: 4

Ingredients:
- *1 tbsp. shallot, diced fine*
- *2 tbsp. apple cider vinegar*
- *1 tbsp. spicy brown mustard*
- *1 tbsp. olive oil*
- *2 tsp. sugar-free maple syrup*

Directions: Place all the ingredients in a small jar with an airtight lid. Shake well to mix. Refrigerate until ready to use.

Nutrition: Calories: 44.7, Carbs: 4.6g, Protein: 0g, Fat: 1.9g, Sugar 0g, Fiber: 0g

159. Pear and Poppy Jam

Preparation Time: 2 hours   **Cooking Time: 30 minutes**
Servings: 32

Ingredients:
- *3 pears, peeled, seeded and chopped*
- *1/2 lemon*
- *3/4 cup Splenda*
- *1 tbsp. poppy seeds*

Directions: Place the pears in a large bowl, sprinkle with Splenda, and toss to coat.
Squeeze the lemon over the pears and toss again. Let sit for 2 hours so the fruit will release its juice.
Place poppy seeds in a medium saucepan over medium heat. Cook, stirring, 1–2 minutes to lightly toast the.
Transfer them to a bowl.
Add the pears with the juice to the saucepan and bring to a boil, stirring frequently. Reduce the heat and let boil 10 minutes or until thickened.
Spoon 1/2 the pears into a blender and process until smooth. Add the puree back to the saucepan along with the poppy seeds. Continue cooking for 10 minutes.
Spoon into 2-pint sized jars with air-tight lids. Let cool completely, screw on the lids, and store in the refrigerator.

Nutrition: Calories: 35.8, Carbs: 7.6g, Protein: 0g, Fat: 0g, Sugar: 5.4g, Fiber: 1g

Smoothies

160. Strawberry Smoothie

Preparation Time: 10 minutes

Servings: 1

Ingredients:
- 1 cup fat-free milk
- 1/3 cup fat-free dry milk powder
- 1/2 cup water
- 1 1/4 cup frozen whole strawberries
- 1 packet granulated Splenda

Directions: Process dry milk, fat-free milk, and water in blender about 15 seconds. Add strawberries and Splenda and blend until smooth.

Nutrition: Calories: 113.7; Fat: 2.1g, Protein: 8.7g, Carbs per 1/2 of recipe: 19.8g

161. Cantaloupe Smoothie

Preparation Time: 11 minutes

Servings: 2

Ingredients:
- 3/4 cup carrot juice
- 4 cups cantaloupe, sliced into cubes
- Pinch salt
- 2 Frozen melon balls
- 1 tsp. chopped fresh basil

Directions: Add the carrot juice and cantaloupe cubes to a blender. Sprinkle with salt.
Process until smooth.
Transfer to a bowl. Chill in the refrigerator for 30 minutes.
Top with the melon balls and basil before serving.

Nutrition: Calories: 134.7, Carbs: 30.8g, Protein: 3.7g, Fat: 0.7g

162. Berry and Spinach Smoothie

Preparation Time: 11 minutes

Servings: 2

Ingredients:
- 2 cups strawberries
- 1 cup raspberries
- 1 cup blueberries
- 1 cup fresh baby spinach leaves
- 1 cup pomegranate juice
- 3 tbsp. milk powder, unsweetened

Directions: Mix all the ingredients in a blender.
Blend until smooth. Chill before serving.

Nutrition: Calories: 117.6, Carbs: 25g, Protein: 4.9g, Fat: 1.2g

163. Tropical Smoothie

Preparation Time: 8 minutes

Servings: 2

Ingredients
- 1 banana, sliced
- 1 cup mango, sliced
- 1 cup pineapple, sliced
- 1 cup peaches, sliced
- 6 oz. non-fat coconut yogurt
- 1/2 cup pineapple wedges

Directions: Freeze the fruit slices for 1 hour.
Transfer to a blender.
Stir in the rest of the ingredients except pineapple wedges.
Process until smooth. Garnish with pineapple wedges.

Nutrition: Calories: 101.7, Carbs: 22.1g, Protein: 2.9g, Fat: 0.5g

164. Watermelon and Cantaloupe Smoothie

Preparation Time: 10 minutes   Servings: 2

Ingredients:
- 1 1/2 cups watermelon, sliced
- 1 cup cantaloupe, sliced
- 1/2 cup nonfat yogurt
- 1/4 cup orange juice

Directions: Add all the ingredients to a blender.
Blend until creamy and smooth. Chill before serving.

Nutrition: Calories: 113.8, Carbs: 12.8g, Protein: 5.1g, Fat: 0.2g

165. Green Detox Smoothie

Preparation Time: 10 minutes   Servings: 4

Ingredients:
- 1 1/2 cups baby spinach
- 2 cups baby kale
- 2 ribs celery, chopped
- 1 medium green apple, chopped
- 1 cup frozen sliced banana
- 1 cup almond milk
- 1 tbsp. grated fresh ginger
- 1 tbsp. chia seeds
- 1 tbsp. honey

Directions: Combine all the ingredients in a blender and blend until smooth.

Nutrition: Calories: 135.8, Fat: 0.8g, Protein: 1.4g, Carbs: 13.2g

166. Detox Smoothie

Preparation Time: 20 minutes   Servings: 4

Ingredients:
- 1/2 avocado
- 1/2 lb. homemade soft-jelly coconut milk
- 1 handful "approved" greens, such as callaloo, watercress, or dandelion greens
- 1 squeeze key lime
- 1 tsp. Dr. Sebi's Bromide Plus Powder

Directions: Mix all the ingredients in a high-speed mixer.
Fill in more water if the mixture is too concentrated.

Nutrition: Calories: 201.7, Fat: 18.9g, Protein: 2.9g, Carbs: 5.9g

167. Banana Chocolate Smoothie

Preparation Time: 10 minutes   Servings: 1

Ingredients:
- 2 cups fat-free milk
- 1 bananas, sliced and frozen
- 3 tablespoons unsweetened cocoa powder
- 2 tablespoons honey
- 1 teaspoon vanilla

Directions: In a blender, combine all the ingredients. Cover and blend until smooth.

Nutrition: Calories: 119.7, Fat: 0.8g, Protein: 5.4g, Carbs per 1/4 of recipe: 22.7g

168. Green Tea Pineapple Smoothie

Preparation Time: 15 minutes   Servings: 1

Ingredients:
- 2 cups frozen unsweetened mixed fruit, preferably peaches and pineapple
- 1 cup cold unsweetened green tea
- 1 tablespoon honey
- 1 tablespoon lemon juice

Directions: Combine fruit, tea, honey and lemon juice in a blender; blend until smooth.

Nutrition: Calories: 105.7, Fat: 0g, Protein: 1.3g, Carbs per 1/2 of recipe: 26.9g

169. Banana Sorbet

Preparation Time: 15 minutes   **Servings: 1**

Ingredients:
- *12 fresh strawberries, chopped*
- *5 bananas, chopped*

Directions: Place strawberries and bananas in separate containers or resealable plastic bags; freeze at least 2 hours or overnight.
Place strawberries in a blender and process until smooth.
Place bananas in a blender and blend until smooth.

Nutrition: Calories: 98.6, Fat: 0g, Protein: 0g, Carbs per 1/6 of recipe: 20.6g

Desserts

170. Honeydew & Ginger Smoothies

Preparation Time: 15 minutes
Servings: 3

Cooking Time: 3 minutes

Ingredients:
- 1 ½ cup honeydew melon, cubed
- ½ cup banana
- ½ cup nonfat vanilla yogurt
- ¼ tsp fresh ginger, grated
- What you'll need from store cupboard:
- ½ cup ice cubes

Directions: Place all Ingredients in a blender and pulse until smooth. Pour into glasses and serve immediately.

Nutrition: Calories: 67.6, Carbs: 15.3g, Protein: 2.6g, Fat 0g, Sugar 11.4g, Fiber 1g

171. Apple Cheesecake

Preparation Time: 5 minutes
Servings: 12

Cooking Time: 15 minutes

Ingredients:

For crust:
- Half cup graham cracker crumbs
- A quarter cup butter, melted
- 2 tablespoons Equal sweetener

For Cheesecake:
- 16 oz reduced-fat cream cheese, softened
- 1 cup Equal sweetener
- 3 cups unsweetened applesauce
- 2 whole eggs
- 2 egg whites
- 2 tablespoons lemon juice
- Two tablespoons cornstarch
- Three fourth tablespoon ground cinnamon
- Half tsp apple pie spice
- One tablespoon vanilla extract
- One cup reduced-fat sour cream

Directions: Preheat the oven to 325°F.

Blend all ingredients for the crust.

Press the mixture into the bottom of a baking pan. Bake for 10 minutes and allow to cool.

Meanwhile, beat the cream cheese and sweetener in a medium-speed mixing bowl until smooth and well mixed. Add eggs, egg whites, applesauce, and lemon juice, and stir. Add the cornstarch, cinnamon, apple pie seasoning, and vanilla, and continue to stir. Fold in sour cream and combine.

Pour the cheesecake combination over the baked crust.

Bake for 45 to 50 minutes. Let the cheesecake cool to room temperature before cover and refrigerate for several hours.

Nutrition: Calories: 196.8, Fat: 11.6g, Carbs: 13.7g, Protein: 6.2g

172.   Cherry and Chocolate Dessert

Preparation Time: 15 minutes   **Cooking Time: 15 minutes**
Servings: 4

Ingredients:
- Two cups fresh cherries
- Two tablespoons artificial sweetener

- One tablespoon level corn flour, blended with one tablespoon cold water

- Low-fat soft cheese
- Two tablespoons skimmed milk
- half level tsp vanilla extract

For the chocolate sauce:
- 1/4 cup dark chocolate, broken into pieces
- One tablespoon unsweetened cocoa powder

- Half tablespoon corn flour, blended with half tbsp cold water
- One tablespoon golden syrup

Directions: Halve the cherries and pit them, reserving 4 entire ones for decoration.

Put 4 tbsp of water and 1 tbsp of the sweetener in a small pot. Simmer until soft for 3-4 minutes.

Mix in the corn flour and cold water and stir in the cherries. Remove from the heat, stirring to prevent the skin from forming.

In a bowl, combine the vanilla extract, cheese, skim milk, and remaining sweetener. Mix well until smooth.

In another bowl, place the dark chocolate chunks, cocoa powder, cornmeal (along with cold water), and golden syrup, to make the chocolate sauce. Heat everything in a small saucepan, stirring constantly, until smooth. Allow to cool, continuing to stir. Add everything into small glasses. Serve each one with a cherry.

Nutrition: Calories: 113.4, Fat: 1.8g, Carbs: 16.4g, Protein: 5.3g, Sugar: 13.7g

173.   Frozen Citrus Cups

Preparation Time: 25 minutes   **Cooking Time: 5 minutes**
Servings: 9 dozen

Ingredients:
- 5 packages (each 3 oz.) of lemon gelatin
- 100 oz. pineapple, cubed
- 55 oz. drained mandarin oranges

- 5 large sliced bananas
- 10 cups of boiling water
- What you will need from the store cupboard:

- 5 cans (each 6 oz.) of frozen orange juice concentrate, thawed partially

Directions: Dissolve the gelatin in boiling water in a large bowl

Keep aside for cooling for 10 minutes. Stir the remaining ingredients in.

Spoon them into your cups. Refrigerate before serving.

Nutrition: Calories: 47.6, Carbs: 11.9g, Fat: 0g, Protein: 1.5g

174.   Chocolate Chip Fat Bomb

Preparation Time: 2 minutes   **Cooking Time: 2 minutes**
Servings: 12

Ingredients:
- 1/2 cup coconut oil

- 1/2 cup no-sugar-added peanut butter

- 2 oz. cream cheese, warmed
- 1/4 cup powdered erythritol

- *1/4 cup low-carb chocolate chips*

Direction: Melt coconut oil in the instant pot on SAUTÉ.
Add cream cheese, erythritol, and peanut butter. Mix well. Pour mixture into silicone baking cups.
Sprinkle the cups with chocolate chips. Freeze before serving.

Nutrition: Calories: 180.7, Fat: 16.1g, Carb: 3.2g, Protein: 3.5g

175. Pecan Clusters

Preparation Time: 5 minutes
Servings: 8

Cooking Time: 5 minutes

Ingredients:
- *3 tbsp. butter*
- *1/4 cup heavy cream*
- *1 tsp. vanilla extract*
- *1 cup pecans, chopped*
- *1/4 cup low-carb chocolate chips*

Directions: Melt the butter on SAUTÉ in the instant pot.
Once the butter is brown, add heavy cream and press CANCEL.
Add the chopped pecans and vanilla. Cool and occasionally stir for 10 minutes.
Line a baking sheet with parchment and spoon mixture on it to form 8 clusters.
Scatter chocolate chips over the clusters. Cool and serve.

Nutrition: Calories: 193.7, Fat: 17.9g, Carbs: 3.8g, Protein: 1.8g

176. Classic Fudge

Preparation Time: 5 minutes
Servings: 10

Cooking Time: 3 minutes

Ingredients
- *1 cup low-carb chocolate chips*
- *8 oz. cream cheese*
- *1/4 cup erythritol*
- *1/4 tsp. cinnamon*
- *1 tsp. vanilla extract*
- *1 cup water*

Directions: Place the erythritol, vanilla, cream cheese, cinnamon, and chocolate chips in a bowl. Cover with foil.
Pour water into the instant pot and place it on the steam rack.
Place the bowl on the rack and cover the lid.
Press the MANUAL bottom and cook for 3 minutes. Do a natural release.
Remove the bowl carefully and stir until smooth.
Line a pan with parchment paper and pour the mixture on it. Chill, slice, and serve.

Nutrition: Calories: 189.7, Fat: 13.2g, Carbs: 8.7g, Protein: 1.7g

177. Lemon Poppy Seed Cake

Preparation Time: 10 minutes
Servings: 6

Cooking Time: 25 minutes

Ingredients:
- *1 cup almond flour*
- *2 eggs*
- *1/2 cup erythritol*
- *2 tsp. vanilla extract*
- *1 tsp. lemon extract*
- *1 tbsp. poppy seeds*
- *4 tbsp. butter, melted*
- *1/4 cup heavy cream*
- *1/8 cup sour cream*
- *1/2 tsp. baking powder*
- *1 cup water*
- *1/4 cup powdered erythritol, for garnish*

Directions: Mix the poppy seeds, erythritol, vanilla, lemon, eggs, and almond flour in a bowl.
Add the baking powder, heavy cream, sour cream, and butter.
Pour into a 7-inch round cake pan and cover with foil.
Pour the water into the instant pot and place it on a steam rack.
Place the cake pan on top of the rack.
Close the lid and press CAKE. Cook for 25 minutes. Do a natural release.
Cool and sprinkle with powdered erythritol.

Nutrition: Calories: 239.7, Fat: 20.1g, Carb: 2.7g, Protein: 3.1g

178. Chocolate Mug Cake

Preparation Time: 5 minutes
Servings: 1
Cooking Time: 20 minutes

Ingredients:
- 1 cup water
- 1/4 cup almond flour
- 2 tbsps. coconut flour
- 1 egg
- 2 tbsps. erythritol
- 1/2 tsp. vanilla extract
- 1 tbsp. butter
- 2 tsps. cocoa powder

Directions: Pour the water into the instant pot and place the steam rack.
Mix the remaining ingredients and mix in a mug. Cover with foil.
Place the mug onto the steam rack and close the lid.
Press the MANUAL and cook for 20 minutes. Do a natural release.
Nutrition: Calories: 383.8, Fat: 28g, Carb: 7.1, Protein: 9.8g

179. Cinnamon Roll Chilled

Preparation Time: 10 minutes
Servings: 1

Ingredients:
- 1 cup unsweetened almond milk
- 2 tablespoons vanilla protein powder
- ½ teaspoon cinnamon
- ¼ teaspoon vanilla extract
- 1 tablespoon chia seeds
- 1 cup ice cubs

Directions: Add listed ingredients to a blender.
Blend until you have a smooth and creamy texture.
Serve chilled.

Nutrition: Calories: 144.7, Fat: 3.8g, Carbs: 1.2g, Protein: 0.9g

180. Toffee Apple Mini Pies

Preparation Time: 5 minutes
Servings: 12
Cooking Time: 25 minutes

Ingredients:
- 2 9-inch pie crusts, soft
- 2 cup Gala apples, diced fine
- 2 tbsp. toffee bits
- 1 tbsp. Splenda
- 1 egg, beaten
- 1 tbsp. butter, cut in 12 cubes
- ½ tsp cinnamon
- Nonstick cooking spray
- 1 ½ tsp fresh lemon juice

Directions: Heat oven to 375 degrees. Spray a cookie sheet with cooking spray.
In a medium bowl, stir together toffee, apples, lemon juice, Splenda, and cinnamon.
Roll pie crusts, one at a time, out on a lightly floured surface.
Cut 12 circles from each crust. Place them on prepared pan.
Brush the dough with half the egg. Spoon 1 tablespoon of the apple mixture on each round, leaving ½- inch edge.
Top with pat of butter. Place second dough round on top and seal edges closed with a fork.
Brush with remaining egg. Bake 25 minutes.
Serve warm.

Nutrition: Calories: 153.7, Carbs: 16.8g, Protein: 1.5g, Fat: 8.7g, Sugar: 5.8g, Fiber 1.2g

181. Sweet Tapioca Pudding

Preparation Time: 10 minutes
Servings: 4
Cooking Time: 8 minutes

Ingredients:
- ½ cup pearl tapioca
- 1 can coconut milk
- ½ cup water
- 4 Tbsp maple syrup
- 1 cup almond milk
- Pinch cardamom

Directions: Soak tapioca in almond milk for 1 hour.
Combine all ingredients except water into the heat-safe bowl and cover the bowl with foil.
Pour ½ cup water into the instant pot, then place trivet into the pot.

Place bowl on top of the trivet.
Cover the pot with the lid and cook on manual high pressure for 8 minutes.
Once done, allow to release pressure naturally, then open the lid.
Stir well, and place in the refrigerator for 1 hour before serving.

Nutrition: Calories: 312.7, Fat: 17.9g, Carbs: 37.9g, Sugar: 18g, Protein: 2.8g

182. Blueberry Cupcakes

Preparation Time: 10 minutes
Servings: 6

Cooking Time: 25 minutes

Ingredients:
- 2 eggs, lightly beaten
- ¼ cup butter, softened
- ½ tsp. baking soda
- 1 tsp. baking powder
- 1 tsp. vanilla extract
- ½ fresh lemon juice
- 1 lemon zest
- ¼ cup sour cream
- ¼ cup milk
- 1 cup sugar
- ¾ cup fresh blueberries
- 1 cup all-purpose flour
- ¼ tsp. salt

Directions: Add all ingredients into the large bowl and mix well.
Empty 1 cup of water into the instant pot, then place trivet into the pot.
Pour batter into the silicone cupcake mound and place it on top of the trivet.
Seal the pot with the lid and cook on manual high pressure for 25 minutes.
Once done, allow to release pressure naturally, then open the lid.

Nutrition: Calories: 329.7, Fat: 11.2g, Carbs: 53.1g, Sugar: 35.8g, Protein: 5.1g

183. Cinnamon Pears

Preparation Time: 10 minutes
Servings: 4

Cooking Time: 7 minutes

Ingredients:
- 4 firm pears, peel
- ½ tsp. nutmeg
- ⅓ cup sugar
- 1 tsp. ginger
- 1 ½ tsp. cinnamon
- 1 cinnamon stick
- 1 cup orange juice

Directions: Add orange juice and all spices into the instant pot.
Place the trivet into the pot and arrange pears on top.
Close the pot with a lid and cook on manual high pressure for 7 minutes.
Once done, allow to release pressure, then open the lid.
Remove pears from the pot and set them aside.
Discard cinnamon sticks and cloves from the pot. Add sugar to the pot and set the pot on sauté mode.
Cook the sauce until thickened. Pour the sauce over pears and serve.

Nutrition: Calories: 220.8, Fat: 0.5g, Carbs: 57.2g, Sugar: 41.9g, Protein: 1.6g

184. Saffron Rice Pudding

Preparation Time: 10 minutes
Servings: 6

Cooking Time: 10 minutes

Ingredients:
- ½ cup rice
- ½ tsp. cardamom powder
- 3 tbsp. almonds, chopped
- 3 tbsp. walnuts, chopped
- 4 cups milk
- ½ cup sugar
- 2 tbsp. shredded coconut
- 1 tsp. saffron
- 3 tbsp. raisins
- 1 tbsp. ghee
- ⅛ tsp. salt
- ½ water

Directions: Add ghee into the pot and set the pot on sauté mode.
Add rice and cook for 30 seconds.
Add 3 cups milk, cardamom powder, coconut, saffron, nuts, raisins, sugar, ½ cup water, and salt, and blend well.
Close the pot with a lid and cook on manual high pressure for 10 minutes.
Once done, release pressure naturally for 15 minutes and then release it using the quick-release method. Open the lid.

Add remaining milk and stir well; cook on sauté mode for 2 minutes.

Nutrition: Calories: 279.6, Fat: 9.3g, Carbs: 41.8g, Sugar: 26.8g, Protein: 8.7g

185.   Vermicelli Pudding

Preparation Time: 10 minutes   **Cooking Time: 2 minutes**
Servings: 6

Ingredients:
- ⅓ cup vermicelli, roasted
- 6 dates, pitted, sliced
- 3 tbsp. cashews, slice
- 2 tbsp. pistachios, slice
- ¼ tsp. vanilla
- ½ tsp. saffron
- ⅓ cup sugar
- 5 cups milk
- 3 tbsp. shredded coconut
- 2 tbsp. raisins
- 3 tbsp. almonds
- 2 tbsp. ghee

Directions: Add ghee to the instant pot and set the pot on sauté mode.
Add dates, pistachios, cashews, and almonds into the pot, and cook for a minute.
Add coconut, raisins, and vermicelli. Stir well. Add 3 cups milk, saffron, and sugar. Blend well.
Close the pot with a lid and cook on manual high pressure for 2 minutes.
Once done, allow to release pressure, then open the lid.
Stir remaining milk and vanilla.

Nutrition: Calories: 282.7, Fat: 13.2g, Carbs: 34.1g, Sugar: 27.6g, Protein: 9.3g

186.   Chocolate Mousse

Preparation Time: 10 minutes   **Cooking Time: 6 minutes**
Servings: 5

Ingredients:
- 4 egg yolks
- ¼ cup water
- ½ cup sugar
- 1 tsp. vanilla
- 1 cup heavy cream
- ½ cup cocoa powder
- ½ cup milk
- ¼ tsp. sea salt

Directions: Whisk egg yolks in a bowl until combined.
In a saucepan, add cocoa, water, and sugar, and whisk over medium heat until sugar is melted.
Add milk and cream to the saucepan and whisk to combine. Do not boil.
Add vanilla and salt; stir well.
Introduce 1 ½ cups water into the instant pot, then place a trivet in the pot.
Pour mixture into the ramekins and place on top of the trivet.
Close the pot with a lid and cook on manual mode for 6 minutes.
Once done, release pressure using the quick-release method, then open the lid. Serve and enjoy.

Nutrition: Calories: 234.7, Fat: 13.8g, Carbs: 26.7g, Sugar: 21g, Protein: 5.2g

187.   Peach Cobbler

Preparation Time: 10 minutes   **Cooking Time: 20 minutes**
Servings: 6

Ingredients:
- 20 oz. can peach pie filling
- 1 ½ tsp. cinnamon
- ¼ tsp. nutmeg
- 14 ½ oz. vanilla cake mix
- ½ cup butter, melted

Directions: Add peach pie filling into the instant pot.
In a bulky container, mix the remaining ingredients and spread them over peach pie filling.
Close the pot with a lid and cook on manual high pressure for 10 minutes.
As soon as done, discharge pressure naturally for 10 minutes and then release it using the quick-release method.

Nutrition: Calories: 444.7, Fat: 14.9g, Carbs: 75.9g, Sugar: 47.1g, Protein: 0.7g

188. Apple Pear Crisp

Preparation Time: 10 minutes
Servings: 4

Cooking Time: 20 minutes

Ingredients:

- 4 apples, peel, and cut into chunks
- 1 cup steel-cut oats
- 2 pears, cut into chunks
- 1 ½ cup water
- ½ tsp. cinnamon
- ¼ cup maple syrup

Directions: Add all ingredients into the instant pot and stir well.
Seal the pot with a lid and cook on manual high for 10 minutes.
Once done, reduce pressure naturally for 10 minutes and then release it using the quick-release method.

Nutrition: Calories: 305.7, Fat: 1.6g, Carbs: 73.8g, Sugar: 44.9g, Protein: 4.1g

Printed in Great Britain
by Amazon

80809233R00047